■ Countries Past, Present or
Potential Candidates for
"Wars of National Liberation"

The Meaning of
Limited War

Robert McClintock

The Meaning of
Limited War

Houghton Mifflin Company Boston
The Riverside Press Cambridge
1967

To Elenita, who went to the wars with me

"The last ten years have taught the world a lesson about how to behave in the grey area between diplomacy and military action. It is only by attending to the rules of escalation, as the Americans and Russians have painfully worked them out, that full-scale war can be avoided. The first of the rules of confrontation is that one should make one's objectives clear, the second that one should do the least that is necessary to achieve them."

The Economist, September 11, 1965

Preface

THE PURPOSE of this book is to study the nature of past, present and probable war in the last half of the twentieth century. Given the strategic atomic stalemate between the megaton powers, the United States and the Soviet Union, and the probability that there will be no recourse to nuclear exchanges as between the Communist Bloc and the Free World, wars of the last half of this much troubled century will be limited in character. The people of the United States, whose sons are currently engaged in the jungles of Indochina, whose troops have landed on the beaches of Beirut, and whose soldiers died in their thousands in the limited war of Korea, have a right to know what they face in the remainder of this millennium.

Living as we do in the "delicate balance of terror," but living more securely because of the immense equilibrium of deterrence which now exists in the world, we will find, paradoxically enough, that large atomic bombs may actually lead to small wars. The megaton powers exist now like scorpions in a bottle, neither daring to sting the other.

Already since the end of World War II, according to one authority,[1] over thirty military engagements have taken place, although possibly not all of these would be termed limited wars. The United States itself, as the leader of the Free World, has been involved either indirectly or directly

in the principal limited wars which have been fought since
the end of World War II. For example, we were involved in
the Greek Civil War which was actually an attempt by the
Communist powers to break into the Mediterranean Sea; we
were very interested spectators in the Israeli-Arab War; we
were the principal participant on the United Nations' side
in the limited war in Korea; we were the main bankers and
logistical backers of the French in the latter aspects of their
war in Indochina, and are now deeply involved ourselves as
protagonists in Viet Nam and Laos; our influence was definitive in the Suez fiasco of 1956; we landed across the
beaches in Lebanon in 1958, killed no one and voluntarily
withdrew; we gave the logistical support to the U.N. military intervention in the Congo in 1960. Therefore no American citizen can fail but be interested to know the nature of
these limited wars which will characterize the last half of
the twentieth century and which will be fought while the
atomic balance of power is maintained.

The literature on the subject of limited war as published
in the United States is prolific and at times bewildering. A
Harvard scholar has brought out an annotated bibliography[2]
which lists more than three hundred articles and books on
the subject of limited war, published since the outbreak of
the Korean conflict. Strangely enough, however, with the
exception of General Maxwell Taylor's book, *The Uncertain
Trumpet*, none of these works seems to have been written
by a professional military man, and no diplomatist has yet
set himself to the task of analyzing the nature of limited war.

Although the bibliography is large, many of the studies
smell of the lamp. There seems to be room for a book to be
written on behalf of the American citizen to set forth in
simple language the nature of limited war in the twentieth
century. The purpose of such a study would be to explain
why we got into the situations we are in and what we are

going to do about it. Because of the paramount power and position of the United States, we will not be able to stay out of limited wars, but at least we should be able to win them, and with a minimum of expenditure of American lives.

The qualifications of the present author are modest. All he can claim is a generation of experience in the American Foreign Service and a number of years spent in that Service during which he personally had experience of limited war. These include the Haitian Massacre in the Dominican Republic in 1937; the "Winter War" in Finland in 1939; the diplomacy which led eventually to a U.N. armistice between Israel and the Arab States in 1947–49; the personal satisfaction of firing a 105 gun-howitzer at the Communist Chinese in Korea in 1952; the experience of being in charge of the U.S. Embassy in Saigon during the battle of Dien Bien Phu in 1954; and a personal participation as "Beachmaster for the Tanks" when the author was the American Ambassador in Lebanon in 1958. Furthermore, as a member of the Policy Planning Staff of the Department of State in 1957, the author submitted a then-secret paper on a "National Doctrine for Limited War" which dared to challenge the existing strategic doctrine of massive retaliation and analyzed for the first time, at least in the diplomatic branch of the United States Government, the nature of limited war. This paper concluded with these words:

> If the precepts established in this paper can be adhered to, there would seem to be a chance for the playing out of limited hostilities for clearly defined and modest objectives without the bringing down upon "civilization" the terminal folly of global war. Ultimately, the principal requirement will be character, and the courage not "to push the button."

This then is a book written by a professional diplomat for the elucidation of the citizen who is concerned. Its purpose will be to show that limited war is political, with the hope that ultimately means can be found without resort to force to resolve political differences between nations.

The emphasis of this study will therefore be on the objectives of limited war and the manner in which eventually these conflicts came to solution. Despite Clemenceau's dictum that "war is far too important to be left to the generals," it is not the intent of this work to second-guess the generals or to provide a military history of limited war. Rather, the stress will be on the diplomacy of force and the force of diplomacy.

This book was written while the author was assigned as the State Department Advisor to the President of the United States Naval War College. There he had extensive access to the archives of the College and to the library dedicated to the memory of Alfred T. Mahan. The author is grateful for the permission given by the United States Naval Institute to use extensive portions of his article on the landings in Lebanon published by them in October 1962.

Contents

The Meaning of
Limited War

CHAPTER I

Limited War and the Development
of U.S. Defense Policy

ONE OF the most famous understatements of history was ut-
terred by Karl von Clausewitz, when he said that "War is
nothing but a continuation of political intercourse with an
admixture of other means." [1]

In a century whose first half was characterized by the two
most terrible and global wars in history, the shell-shocked
citizen frequently disregards the essential fact of limited war,
which is that it is fought for political objectives. Up until
the outbreak of the first of the two world wars, previous conflicts were kept limited in their geographic extent and in the
objectives of the participants. [2] The two world wars, however, amounted to civil wars of humanity — race fratricide.
They ended in the downfall of empires and the ultimate division of the world into Communist camp and free, with a
third element made up of the non-aligned nations. The Second World War likewise led to the development of the atomic
bomb and the balance of terror, the strategic deterrent, the
pax ballistica.

With the development of hydrogen megaton bombs, the
consequences of total war become too lethal for serious statesmen to contemplate, unless in the increasingly improbable
context of a completely successful surprise attack. The question of military "victory" enters the equation with increasing reservations. The emphasis becomes one of sur-

vival. A peace without victory might be tolerable, but a peace without survival would be meaningless. Therefore, we come to the second half of this troubled twentieth century in which the paradox of bigger atomic bombs makes possible the conduct of small wars.* Within the nuclear boxing ring rounds can be fought without blowing up the whole arena.

Not all of this rationale has always been seen clearly. After the end of World War II, when the United States still had a monopoly of the atomic bomb, our defense doctrine was based on the concept of "massive retaliation." As General Maxwell Taylor has pointed out, "our own people were quick to believe that our armed forces had in the air-delivered atomic bomb the absolute weapon which would permit the United States, its sole possessor, to police the world through the threat of its use." [4]

The American Secretary of Defense spoke blithely of getting "a bigger bang for the buck";† and our military leaders, with the exception of the Army, went over enthusiastically to the atomic concept. The author well remembers attending a conference on limited war staged in 1957 by the U.S. Air Force in which the generals bitterly lamented the requirement imposed upon them to retain conventional bomb racks in their aircraft, so eager were they to go all-nuclear. When

* "It would seem, therefore, as if there is now an almost complete deterrent system: the striking forces balance each other and therefore act as a deterrent against an all-out nuclear struggle; the conventional forces act as a deterrent against limited war, since the ever-present risks of escalation will be a deterrent against entering upon limited war for any too important a stake. The effectiveness of these three forms of action depends to a great extent upon the factor of uncertainty but, complementing each other and welded into a unified system, they make an overall balance possible."

However, "The deterrent . . . has no power to prevent action in the political and economic field, or utilization of revolutionary movements in foreign countries, or even war conducted by proxy."

Général d'Armée André Beaufre: *An Introduction to Strategy*, p. 85.[3]

† The cap-pistol equivalent of this cliché in those days, when Washington sought to do difficult things cheaply and easily, was "psychological warfare."

he queried the then Chief of Staff of the Air Force if he actually thought nuclear fire-power could deal with a guerrilla war situation like that in Malaya, the General merely responded, "Yes."

It was once observed that one of the defects of the Spanish character was the *sentido del honor*, an exaggerated pride, an overdevelopment of the feeling of personal honor to the point where life itself would be placed at stake for the most trivial slight or imagined offense. There is a certain similarity between the Spanish *sentido del honor* and readiness to fight to the death for any infringement of personal honor, and the United States' professed readiness to risk national suicide by using "massive retaliation" to prevent or influence purely local conflict.

However, the outbreak of war in Korea forced sober people to think sober thoughts. With Clausewitz at the back of their brains, the leaders of American policy decided on political grounds not to employ the atomic weapon. Only a month after the outbreak of the Korean War an editorial appeared in the *Bulletin of the Atomic Scientists*, warning that the next decade was likely to be marked by a series of "small wars waged by satellite armies" in which the atomic bomb would be of no value. The editorial urged that the United States should therefore develop large and adequately equipped mobile land forces.[5]

In October 1957, Sputnik was launched by the U.S.S.R. The Russian superiority in ballistic missiles caused the United States to doubt if the "balance of terror" could in fact be maintained. The Gaither Report was written. Much dither was made of the so-called missile gap. Although the Eisenhower Administration talked about the need to have a capability for limited or conventional war, with its decision to limit defense budgets it perforce put its money into the strategic forces.

However, toward the end of the Eisenhower administrations there was much less talk of "massive retaliation." President Eisenhower had witnessed the end of the French limited war in Indochina; he had exerted massive influence in terminating the Anglo-French-Israeli adventure at Suez; and he had undertaken a successful exercise in limited war in the American landings in Lebanon. Meanwhile, the Army Chief of Staff, General Maxwell Taylor, thought the issue worth his own resignation in order to hammer his thesis of the need for a doctrine of flexible response as the basis of our military policy. To General Taylor it was evident that the United States and the U.S.S.R. were existing in a framework of mutual deterrence and that therefore there was need for a reappraisal of the requirements for limited war.[6]

The rethinking and reformation of American defense policy was brilliantly summed up in the message which President Kennedy sent to the Congress on the defense budget on March 28, 1961. Here it is sufficient to quote only the opening lines of paragraph one:

> The primary purpose of our arms is peace, not war — to make certain that they will never have to be used — to deter all wars, general or limited, nuclear or conventional, large or small — to convince all potential aggressors that any attack would be futile — to provide backing for diplomatic settlement of disputes — to insure the adequacy of our bargaining power for an end to the arms race. The basic problems facing the world today are not susceptible to a military solution.

And so, although it is usual at the outset to commence by definitions, this chapter concludes with a definition of limited war.

Up until 1959 the official Pentagon definitions of general war and limited war were as follows:

> General war is a conflict in which the forces of the United States and the USSR are directly involved and in which atomic weapons are assumed to be used from the outset.

> Limited war is a conflict short of general war in which United States forces will use atomic weapons as required to achieve national objectives.[7]

The present author's own definition of limited war is as follows:

> Limited war is a conflict short of general war to achieve specific political objectives, using limited forces and limited force. As between the great nuclear powers, the maintenance of the global strategic nuclear balance of power would preclude the use of strategic nuclear weapons, and fear of escalation would inhibit the use of tactical nuclear weapons.

To this the Office of the Assistant Secretary of Defense (International Security Affairs) made the following comment:

> Limited war in the formal terminology of the U.S. military services refers to an "armed conflict short of general war, exclusive of incidents, involving the overt engagement of the military forces of two or more nations." The Ambassador used the term to include guerrilla and unconventional warfare which are separate and distinct JCS terms as described in JCS Pub 1, "Dictionary of U.S. Military Terms for Joint Usage," 1 Feb. 1964.

By all means, let our military leaders retain their definitions. The concerned citizen will also read with a mixture of confidence and challenge Khrushchev's speech of January 6, 1961, to the twenty-second Communist Congress, which outlined a twenty-year strategy of "anti-imperialist national liberation revolutions"; and the blueprint for disaster of Mao Tse-tung as paraphrased by his Minister of Defense, Marshal Lin Piao, on September 2, 1965, which translated into Communist Chinese the concept of "wars of national liberation."

CHAPTER II

The Varieties of Limited War

THAT THE WORLD had entered upon the *pax ballistica* there could be no doubt after 1960. The lonely radar vigils on the DEW Line and at Thule, the instant readiness of SAC, the deployment of ever-moving airfields at sea in the great attack carriers, stood off a lesser Soviet capability in airborne strategic bombing and a closely estimated capability to launch intercontinental ballistic missiles against the United States. Meanwhile American advances in the science of solid propellents made possible Minute Man and the Polaris missile. Minute Man rockets in hardened silos were almost invulnerable to atomic counterattack, but could still be located by enemy intelligence; only a question mark of foam curling in the sea above a FBM* submarine punctuated the mystery of its presence. The *pax ballistica* seemed secure.

The world entered now upon what future historians may some day describe as the *pax guerrilla*. As indicated in the Preface, since the end of World War II one authority has discerned no less than thirty-two military engagements for political ends. Whether one lists those engagements vertically in chronological sequence of time or horizontally in making a voyage around the world, the list is impressive. Even if one starts this *tour d'horizon* at the center of our world, the American schoolboy's map which always puts the Western Hemisphere in the middle, there is little cause for complacency.

* Fleet Ballistic Missile.

Since the end of World War II there have been revolutions in fourteen of the twenty American Republics.*

Moving west across the broad Pacific, we find the nations of Asia embroiled in limited wars: the war in Korea; the continuing war in Viet Nam; the Communist struggle to take Laos; the Hukbalahap insurrection in the Philippines; the scuffles in the Taiwan Straits between Nationalist Chinese and Communist Chinese; the Indonesian struggle for independence, its subsequent taking of West Irian and its attacks on Malaysia; the long drawn out Malayan guerrilla war; and, moving further west, China's occupation of Tibet and its subsequent attack on the Himalayan frontier of India; the Indian excision of the Portuguese enclave at Goa; and the conflicts between Pakistan and India in Kashmir and the Rann of Kutch, to say nothing of the full-scale fighting near Lahore which broke out in the autumn of 1965.

Moving further to the west there was the brief British intervention at Kuwait to forestall an Iraqi takeover, the coup d'état in Baghdad which destroyed the Iraqi royal family and led to the American landing in Lebanon, the Israeli-Arab war, the episode at Suez, and the guerrilla war in Cyprus which has now turned into civil war. Along the coast of North Africa in the Maghreb there were hostilities between France and Tunisia, the long drawn out Algerian war for independence, and a brief but bloody border skirmish between Morocco and Algeria. South of the Sahara there was the United Nations intervention in the Congo and the current revolt in that vast heartland of Africa, leaving aside such exercises in violence, if not limited war, as a coup d'état in the Sudan, an attempt to dethrone the Emperor of Ethiopia, and the recent military seizures of power in West and Central Africa. The Portuguese were also busy in Angola attempting

---

* Argentina, Bolivia, Brazil, Colombia, Costa Rica, Cuba, Dominican Republic, Ecuador, Guatemala, Haiti, Honduras, Panama, Peru, Venezuela.

to stamp out the flames of revolution stirred up by Holden Roberto.

Lord Attlee once remarked that there is a great release of political energy when new nations are born. There is a curious relationship between the incidence of limited war in the second half of the twentieth century and the emergence of the new nations. For example, of the conflicts just outlined in Asia, fourteen new sovereignties have emerged since World War II and thirteen of these new countries were involved in limited war. The record for the Near East is even more unanimous: five new nations, all five involved in various limited wars. The record is better in Africa where thirty-three new nations have emerged since 1945 and only six were involved in limited war (revolutions and military coups are disregarded in this computation). However, the new countries of Africa benefited from the wisdom of the British Raj in deciding to liquidate the British Empire on civilized terms; and by the *Logique Française* which drew stern but implacable conclusions from the battle of Dien Bien Phu — perhaps the most important political battle to be fought in the twentieth century. It was in consequence of Dien Bien Phu that France decided on the orderly liquidation of its African Empire and De Gaulle seized the nettle of Algerian independence, thus losing Algiers but saving France. Even in our own supposed area of the *Pax Americana,* the garden of the Alliance for Progress, as noted above, fourteen revolutions have taken place since World War II and one revolution, in Cuba, made that country a focus of Communist infection in the hemisphere. However, although some revolutions assume the aspects of limited war (e.g., the deployment of an army corps in Argentina against the rebel naval base of Puerto Belgrano in 1963), revolution in the Latin American or African sense is excluded from the scope of this study. "Wars of national liberation" are, alas, horses of another color: frequently pink, generally red.

These happenings in far-off places may seem remote to the American man in the street, but the concerned citizen should indeed be concerned. The United States is tied by military and political alliances approved by the voters through their senatorial representation in such instruments as the Organization of American States, the NATO (North Atlantic Treaty Organization), the SEATO (Southeast Asia Treaty Organization), the ANZUS pacts linking us with Australia and New Zealand, and bilateral defense agreements with Korea, Japan, Taiwan, the Philippines, and Iran. We are likewise members of that peaceful pact, the Colombo Plan, and "observers" in the Baghdad Pact devoid of Baghdad, now called CENTO, the Central Treaty Organization. In addition there is a vast nexus of military aid bilateral agreements providing for military advisory groups. There are many base agreements still in existence and there are still the unrevoked Truman and Eisenhower Doctrines, the first of world-wide implications. And finally, there is the most encompassing treaty of them all, to which the United States is a leading party — the Charter of the United Nations.

In consequence the "concerned citizen" looks at a world map pockmarked by a score and a half of limited wars which have been fought or are being fought in the first score of years since World War II ended. Furthermore, the *pax guerrilla* has taken on a new and sinister aspect since Khrushchev in his speech of January 6, 1961, first gave world-wide publicity to the descriptive phrase, "wars of national liberation." Although the *pax ballistica* might keep the strategic balance in preventing nuclear exchanges between the megaton powers, the Communists found that by resorting to "wars of national liberation" — to guerrilla wars for political objectives — they might sap the foundations and the fortress of the Free World by subversion from within. Thus far the Free World has not yet developed a common view on how to deal with wars of national liberation and there is no common strategy, nor any agreed method for dealing with this ubiquitous and insidious threat.

However, wars of national liberation are not the only kind of limited wars which have been fought in the last twenty years, nor are they the only kind which will perhaps be fought in future. It is necessary to an understanding of limited war to review the seven categories in which these conflicts may be classified. There is *limited strategic war* as in the case of Greece and Korea. There are *simple wars for independence* as in the instance of Israel, Algeria, and Cyprus. We can leave aside pure or impure *domestic rebellion,* as for example in the American republics, but must recognize a category of *civil war with outside intervention* for obvious political objectives. Such a case will be studied in Lebanon. Then, there are *wars for the simple acquisition of territory,* such as the conflict for Kashmir and the Chinese attack on the Himalayan frontier of India. A sixth category is thus far *sui generis — wars fought for limited political and strategic objectives,* such as the episode at Suez. And finally there are the "wars of national liberation" *par excellence:* Viet Nam, French style, and Viet Nam, American style.

There is an additional category of limited engagement which some authorities might include under the rubric of limited war. This would include Berlin and Cuba. However, to the present writer it would seem that the confrontation in Berlin and the "eyeball-to-eyeball" stance over the Soviet placing of nuclear ballistic missiles in Cuba in 1962 were limited exercises in general war rather than general exercises in limited war.

Perhaps of greatest interest in our study will be the so-called "wars of national liberation." Here we must tread warily when we talk of "counterinsurgency," because citizens of the United States are inheritors of the American Revolution. We must also keep in mind that when the colonies fought the parent Great Britain in 1776 there was likewise foreign intervention, in this case, the active participation of French naval and military power, with passive Spanish intervention in the joint cause against England. We should distinguish in discussing "wars of national liberation" between such limited struggles and the cataclysmic revolutions of class against class, such as the French Revolution and the Russian. These were far from "limited war," and their unlimited effects have shaped the course of history.

However, a new category, or at least a new jargon of "wars of national liberation" has emerged in the mouths and writings of the Communist leadership. In fact, one of the tragedies of our time is that the aspirations of men to be free should be made a travesty of by those whose profession it is to enslave. It is likewise clear from watching the antics of certain leaders of nationalist movements that there is much truth in Dr. Johnson's dictum that "Patriotism is the last refuge of a scoundrel."

If we analyze, however, the nature of limited war in the last half of the twentieth century, it is easy to see that a number of wars of so-called "national liberation" have been fought. As indicated above, these include the continuing conflicts in Indochina, the Greek Civil War (although its main objective was strategic), the guerrilla war in Malaya, the Hukbalahap insurrection in the Philippines, the conflict in Indonesia against the Dutch Colonial Government, and the war of independence of Algeria. In each case, the Communist High Command participated in aiding, abetting, and seeking victory for the insurrectionists against the established order. In the case of Malaya, the Philippines and Greece, the Communist side did not succeed, and recent events in Indonesia suggest a decisive Communist defeat. Algeria is independent and not yet subservient to Communist dominance.

There have been other incipient wars of "national liberation," but not at all to suit the purpose of the Communist Bloc. These included the tragic Hungarian Rebellion of 1956 and the equally unsuccessful and tragic, though less known, rebellion in Tibet in 1959, both of which resulted in a reaffirmation of Communist domination.

In the ensuing chapters an attempt will be made to examine in some detail these various categories of limited war and to relate in particular their political objectives and the means used to obtain them. Later, an attempt will be made to draw some general conclusions on the nature of limited war in this last half of the twentieth century, including also a regard for the position of the United Nations and of the organized international community in dealing with the problem of limited war.

Obviously, the reader would grow weary of a meticulous narration of the thirty or more engagements fought for political objectives which have taken place since World War II. It should suffice, therefore, in considering the first category of limited strategic war, because this borders closest to the peril of general war, to take up the cases of Greece and Korea.

An important illustration of a limited war for independence is that of Israel versus the Arab states. Limited war for specific political and strategic objectives can be characterized by the Israeli-French-British attack at Suez. A case study in civil war with outside intervention, and involving the landing of American forces, is that of Lebanon. As for a war for the acquisition of territory, we shall examine the Chinese-Indian struggle on the Himalayan frontier.

And finally, in the category of "wars of national liberation," the study will close with a consideration of the wars in Indochina, and particularly Viet Nam. These will be "Viet Nam — French Style" and "Viet Nam — American Style." Perhaps by the time this book is published there will hopefully be a "Viet Nam — New Style."

CHAPTER III

The Civil War in Greece, 1946–1949

1.

ALTHOUGH GREEKS refer to the civil conflict between the Communist guerrillas and the royal government as the Symmorito-Polemo, a gangster or bandit war, and feel very strongly against calling the conflict a civil war, nevertheless, the struggle in Greece was far more than a gangster episode. It was one of the most important wars which have taken part in the second half of this century. The conflict in Greece was the strategic expression of a centuries-old Russian objective: the Slavic drive to warm seas. The Soviet Union already possessed Communist satellites on the Adriatic in Albania and Yugoslavia, while Bulgaria threatened Thrace. If Greece could be made a satellite, the Aegean would become a Communist lake and Turkey, the guardian of the Straits and the entrance to the Black Sea, would be outflanked; therefore, the Symmorito-Polemo, although a limited war using limited forces and limited force, had as its specific goal Russian access to the Mediterranean.

There are other aspects of interest in studying the limited war in Greece. Here, for the first time, there was the use on both sides, the U.S.S.R. and the U.S., of surrogate troops — other people's soldiers to fight the strategic battle.

The conflict in Greece likewise inaugurated new basic

American defense policies which were to have lasting historical impact in the development of the twentieth century. It
was from the conflict in Greece that the Truman Doctrine
was born; it was from the Truman Doctrine that the Marshall
Plan evolved; and a direct military corollary of the Marshall
Plan was the North Atlantic Treaty.

Furthermore, from our experience in Greece, Americans
learned the hard way by their own and others' mistakes. The
United States commenced, in its experience of the Greek
civil war, the evolution of a concept for the management of
our affairs overseas by what later came to be known as the
"Country Team." This was the evolution of an integrated
operational mechanism for the application of American foreign policy in given situations abroad. The development of
American aid for Greece and the diplomatic conduct of our
policy in the Greek Civil War form object lessons from which
conclusions will later be drawn when we study the present
functioning of the Country Team.

The origins of the Communist attempt to take over Greece
go back far beyond the day when German forces left the
peninsula and were replaced by British troops. Even so early
as June 1944, a Soviet military mission had been dispatched
to the mountains of northern Greece after deliberate decep-
tion of the British authorities.[1]

On December 3, 1944, the ELAS revolt broke out in Athens
over the issue of disarming partisan guerrilla fighters. The
Communist ELAS forces took over northern Greece and
Macedonia, while 40,000 British troops held Athens and the
Peloponnesus. An uneasy truce was negotiated and the Varkiza Agreement was signed on February 12, 1945, providing
that both the Communist ELAS and the Loyalist EP forces
be demobilized and disarmed. Hostages were to be released,
an amnesty proclaimed, and a plebiscite to be held in 1945
on a new Greek Constitution.[2] Under the Varkiza truce,

events jogged along uneasily in Greece, the sanction of British power preserving in the interim the integrity of the State.

2.

However, the Communists had already tipped their hand and it was apparent that the Soviet drive toward the Mediterranean had only been averted. Guerrilla warfare continued in the north and on December 3, 1946, Greece complained formally to the United Nations Security Council that Albania, Bulgaria, and Yugoslavia were giving refuge to Greek fugitives from justice and allowing the Communist guerrillas to use their territory as a base for operations in northern Greece.

The Security Council, on December 19, 1946, established a Commission of Investigation made up of representatives of all eleven members of the Council. Its report, issued in May 1947, found that Yugoslavia, and to a lesser extent Albania and Bulgaria, had supported the Communist rebels in the civil conflict in Greece. In some detail, the Commission of Investigation reported that Yugoslavia had recruited, trained, supplied, and dispatched rebels to Greece to fight against the legitimate government; and that special camps had been set up in Bulkes in Yugoslavia and in Rubic in Albania, for political indoctrination of the guerrillas. In addition, the Commission found that both the Bulgarian and Yugoslav governments had encouraged the growth of a separatist movement which had as its object the establishment of an independent Macedonia.[3]

The investigating commission's report was not signed by the Russian and Polish delegates, and the French representative abstained. The Security Council got nowhere in the discussion of the report, and eventually the United Nations General Assembly in 1947 established a special Balkan Committee called UNSCOB, to observe the degree to which the four governments concerned carried out the recommendations of the Security Council's Commission of Investigation. From the outset the Albanian, Bulgarian and Yugoslav governments refused permission for the Committee to maintain observers inside their territories and therefore UNSCOB could only operate from Greece, where it arrived at the end of November 1947. Nevertheless, the formal conclusion of the Balkan Committee's report made it unmistakably clear that the rebels had been receiving aid from Albania, Yugoslavia, and Bulgaria in the form of war materials, use of their territory for tactical operations, and facilities for rest and hospitalization.[4]

3.

While the guerrilla war continued, and even before the official reports of the United Nations pointed to the complicity of the Communist states in attacking the integrity and independence of Greece, it became evident in Washington that the British could no longer continue to carry the burden. As early as the autumn of 1945, the British Government had suggested that it would like American assistance in Greece, especially financial help to the Greek Government.[5]

Early in 1947, on February 3, U.S. Ambassador MacVeagh telegraphed from Athens that the British Forces might withdraw from Greece;[6] and on the 18th of that month, Mark Ethridge, the American Representative on the Security Council investigating commission, warned that all signs pointed to an impending move by the Communists to seize the country. Two days later, the American Embassy in London telegraphed that the British Treasury was opposing any further aid to Greece because of the precarious financial situation in which the United Kingdom found itself;[7] and on the 21st

of February the British Ambassador asked to see Secretary of
State Marshall, who was out of town, but left a copy of a
note which indicated that the United Kingdom would have
to pull its forces out of Greece no later than the last day of
March.[8]

The masters of the Kremlin in plotting their designs for
egress to the Mediterranean can surely have had no con-
templation of the vast chain of political consequences to
which their action gave rise.

The American Government very quickly perceived the nature and dimension of the threat. As President Truman has
put it in his memoirs, "Greece needed aid, and needed it
quickly and in substantial amounts. The alternative was the
loss of Greece and the extension of the Iron Curtain across
the Eastern Mediterranean. If Greece was lost, Turkey
would become an untenable outpost in a sea of Communism.
Similarly, if Turkey yielded to Soviet demands, the position
of Greece would be extremely endangered."

Forced by the catalyst of British withdrawal from Greece,
the American Government moved swiftly. President Truman
carefully prepared the ground with Congressional leaders,
asking them for initial increments of aid in the amount of
$250,000,000 for Greece and $150,000,000 for Turkey. The
President then enunciated that statement of policy which almost immediately became associated with his name — the
Truman Doctrine. As the President has stated, "This was, I
believe, the turning point in America's foreign policy, which
now declared that wherever aggression, direct or indirect,
threatened the peace, the security of the United States was
involved." [9]

In his message to Congress, President Truman declared,
"It must be the policy of the United States to support free
peoples who are attempting to resist subjugation by armed
minorities or by outside pressures." He went on, "I believe

that we must assist free peoples to work out their own destinies in their own way.

"I believe that our help should be primarily through economic and financial aid, which is essential to economic stability and orderly political processes." [10]

If anyone in the Kremlin had a sense of history, he must have read with a certain sense of irony the quotation made by President Truman in his Jefferson Day speech, April 5, 1947, when he was enlisting popular support for aid for Greece and Turkey. In his speech, the President quoted from Jefferson's letter to Monroe urging the adoption of what later became known as the Monroe Doctrine — a doctrine whose genesis was in large part due to the American reaction to imperial Russian encroachment down the west coast of the North American continent. Jefferson wrote Monroe, "Nor is the occasion to be slighted which this proposition offers of declaring our protest against the atrocious violations of the rights of nations by interference by anyone in the internal affairs of another." [11]

In other words, the Russians, once more on the move, and seeking access to the warm seas, had once more aroused American resistance clothed in action. As indicated above, the Truman Doctrine led directly to the Marshall Plan, which in turn led to NATO. The Soviet Union, therefore, in its limited war for a strategic objective in the Aegean had commenced a chain reaction of the widest historical significance. Its "limited war" had unlimited consequences.

4.

It was perhaps more than coincidence that when President Truman signed the Greek-Turkish aid bill on May 22, 1947, on the following day the United Nations' Balkan Investigating Committee had formally concluded that Yugoslavia, Bulgaria and Albania were supporting the uprising against the Greek Government. It was surely no coincidence that immediately after the passage of the Greek-Turkish aid bill, the Communist rebels, aided from outside, stepped up their efforts to win a final victory in Greece.[12]

To meet the threat and with the passage of the Greek-Turkish aid bill, the United States Government moved quickly. Paul Porter, formerly head of OPA, who had been appointed by President Truman as Chief of the Economic Mission to Greece,[13] was replaced by the former Governor of Nebraska, Dwight P. Griswold, who was named Administrator of the Greek Aid Program.[14] On the day the President signed the Greek-Turkish aid bill the acting chief of a new military group, an army colonel, with six other military personnel, left for Greece by air.[15] They reported to the civilian Chief of the U.S. Mission to Greece, generally called AMAG. Major General William G. Livesay, the new Chief of the United States Military Group, USAGG, arrived in Athens on June 16, 1947.[16]

The initial setup of the American aid effort for Greece satisfied no one. There were in effect two senior U.S. representatives in Athens — the American Ambassador, Lincoln MacVeagh, and Governor Griswold, the head of the aid mission. His military chief, General Livesay, was limited in his contact with the Greek military authorities to the strictly passive role of a non-voting observer for logistical matters. In fact, the cat's cradle of conflicting authority became so urgently confused that Major General S. J. Chamberlin was dispatched in the fall of 1947 to survey the situation. In the so-called Chamberlin Report it was recommended that a single civilian diplomat represent the U.S. Government in Athens, rather than the United States Ambassador and chief of the aid mission reporting separately to the Department of State with neither having authority over the other. General

Chamberlin also recommended that "a U.S. Advisory and Planning Group be established, with the authority to advise the U.S. Ambassador and to furnish the Greek authorities high level military advice." By the end of the year, both recommendations were adopted.[17]

That there was confusion as to the powers and jurisdiction of Ambassador and aid mission chief may have been due to the fact that the basic legislation was exceedingly brief in authorizing the mechanism of U.S. aid to Greece. Public Law 75 of May 22, 1947, did require coordination of all U.S. agencies participating in the program, but did not further specify how this coordination would be carried out in the field. It is clear, however, from the testimony of the Executive agencies before the House and Senate that only small advisory missions were originally contemplated. However, as is apparently usual in these cases of Parkinson's Law taking over, the aid mission to Greece soon had 70 per cent more staff members than originally contemplated. Its chief was given very widespread authority "to determine and supervise the programs of American aid including the terms and conditions" under which aid would be given to the Greek Government. A subsequent qualification that the mission chief should be subordinate to the judgments of the Ambassador on political matters was insufficient to define clearly the supremacy of one chief over the other. This conflict of authority was eventually straightened by fiat from the National Security Council; and the final phase began on July 18, 1948, when the new American Ambassador was charged with coordinating authority over the whole aid program.

Pursuant to the Chamberlin Report, a new military mechanism was set up, called the Joint United States Military Advisory and Planning Group — Greece, with the cumbersome abbreviated and unpronounceable name of JUSMAPG. This entity was established by a joint directive on December

31, 1947.[18] However, in these days of trial and error and groping for more effective solutions to obdurate problems, perfection had not yet been achieved. For example, the individual service groups in JUSMAPG were not under the command of the Director, who therefore could not enforce their cooperation in a showdown without reference to Washington. Nevertheless, with the establishment of JUSMAPG, U.S. officers were at last permitted to advise the Greek Government on operational matters in addition to logistics.[19]

5.

Despite the emphasis in the Truman Doctrine on aid, primarily in the economic and financial sense of the term, the deteriorating military situation soon caused the Department of State early in 1948 to decide that "Reconstruction in Greece must take second priority to establishing military security and the elimination of the guerrillas." [20]

No better man to implement this new policy directive could have been found than Lieutenant General James A. Van Fleet, who arrived in Greece on February 24, 1948, to take over from General Livesay as Director of JUSMAPG and as the Commanding General of the U.S. Army Group — Greece, USAGG.

General Van Fleet came at a difficult time. Morale in the Greek fighting forces was at very low ebb. Furthermore, the military direction of the war was under constant harassment by the Greek politicians. Each Minister had his own village or villages for which he claimed special protection. For example, initially forty-seven of the eighty battalions of the Greek Army were tied up in static village guard duty as a result of these political pressures.[21]

Since this is a study of the diplomacy of limited war, here it is appropriate to mention briefly the interrelationships between the British and American military missions working together in Greece to maintain the integrity of the kingdom. As we know, it was the British who held the main burden after VE-Day for assisting Greece to defend itself against its indigenous Communist guerrillas, trained and organized in the three Communist countries along the northern frontier. With the departure of the British troops there still remained behind four military missions and a combat unit of 1200 troops. The four missions were military (Army, Navy, RAF, and a group to counsel on police and prison management). Thanks to devotion and good will on both sides, the American and British military components coordinated their activities successfully. In January 1948, agreements were worked out which in substance provided that the U.S. was to advise on supply, logistical, and operational matters, while the British were to advise on organization and training. However, "All questions which concerned the general efficiency and political character of the Greek forces were to be the joint responsibility of both the U.S. and the British." [22]

Ten days before the arrival of General Van Fleet, on St. Valentine's Day, representatives of the American and British Embassies and AMAG met with the Greek Prime Minister and members of his Cabinet. A memorandum was presented to the Prime Minister which expressed concern over the disorganization in the Greek Military High Command and the failure of the Greek Army to initiate a major offensive against the guerrillas. Specifically, it was recommended that the guerrilla bands must be broken up within six months if the survival of Greece as a sovereign state was to be assured. The Chief of AMAG should be present at meetings of the Supreme National Defense Council. The preparations and carrying out of military plans must be entrusted to the military authorities without political interference. And basically, "unquestioned military authority must be given to one top military commander." [23] This memorandum was speedily elaborated in a so-called "Gentlemen's Agreement."

The difficulties which General Van Fleet faced were formidable. In addition to the political pressure on the military leadership, which has been pointed out above, there was a general feeling of malaise and low morale in all ranks of the Greek Army. There was lack of good leadership in the officer corps, attributable largely to the failure to reward the competent and to eliminate poor leaders. Existing laws made it very difficult to replace inefficient officers and there was no provision for advancing outstanding junior and field grade officers by promotion.[24] Furthermore, the guerrillas were exceedingly tough fighters, aided by an equally tough terrain. They had an open sanctuary along the northern border; and access to supplies and training in Albania, Yugoslavia, and Bulgaria, over whose frontiers, as one British observer put it, "the elaborate etiquette of the Cold War forbade the Government's troops to pursue them." [25]

However, General Van Fleet persisted. He made it a policy to pay personal visits to the Greek units. Good example led to emulation, and the Greek General Staff began to follow Van Fleet's lead. This personal touch resulted in higher morale and quickening of the spirit of combat in the Greek armed forces. Nevertheless, despite the gentlemen's agreement signed in February 1948, the Spring offensive did not succeed; and, as one observer trenchantly put it, "As the year wore on, the agreement wore out." [26]

The combined pressure of events at last led to the appointment of a Supreme Commander with full power to conduct the war. General Alexander Papagos, who had defeated the Italians eight years before, was recalled from retirement and appointed Commander in Chief on January 20, 1949.[27] An emergency law passed the same day granted every authority needed by a real Commander in Chief of all the armed forces.[28]

6.

At the same time as the loyalist forces were gradually evolving with United States aid and advice into an effective fighting team and, at long last, had found a Commander in Chief with full powers, a windfall leading to certain Free World victory transpired on the Communist side. In late 1948 the Yugoslav sanctuary for the Greek guerrillas was withdrawn and eventually the frontier was closed. As one writer has put it, "It is not necessary to assume that Communists never commit errors of judgment." [29]

Put in shorthand form, as the distinguished *New York Times* commentator, C. L. Sulzberger, wrote on February 24, 1965, "The Greek Rebellion was not a pure guerrilla, but a kind of formal war, based in Albania and defeated when Yugoslavia quit the rebel sponsors." Mr. Sulzberger also had a neat quotation from Talleyrand which aptly applied to the Communist denials of intervention in the Greek Civil War: "non-intervention is a political and metaphysical term and means about the same as intervention."

The defection of Yugoslavia was a mistake made in Moscow. In June 1948, the Cominform denounced Tito for various heresies. A violent propaganda campaign ensued from Moscow, echoed in the capitals of the Soviet satellites, and a commercial boycott was imposed on Yugoslavia. The reason for the excommunication of Tito was the Soviet fear that the army and administrative bureaucracy of Yugoslavia might be unreliable as judged from the central Communist point of view because they had been created by Tito, forged in war under his leadership, and owed their first loyalty to him.[30]

Another mistake made in Moscow was the announcement in February 1949 by the Cominform of its intent to create "an independent Macedonian state out of the relevant areas of Greece, Yugoslavia, and Bulgaria." The Communist forces working against Greece were therefore split between so-called nationalist deviationists and the true faithful.[31]

The capstone of this intra-Communist quarrel came on July 10, 1949 when Tito, in a speech at Pola, announced the closing of the Greco-Yugoslav frontier.[32]

The end was now in sight. The Communist guerrillas had several times sought and failed to capture sufficient territory in northern Greece to justify the claim of having established a "free Greece" to which partisans could rally. Thus in January 1949, they captured and held Karpenisi for eighteen days; and in February attacked Florina with 4000 men, supported by 75 mm. and 105 mm. artillery. This last major effort in the whole Civil War ended in total defeat. It was a mistake on the part of the Communists to leave guerrilla warfare tactics for the more classical simple assault.[33]

Finally, General Papagos' terminal campaign in the Gramos Massif led in the late summer and autumn of 1949 to the capture of the Communist headquarters of "General" Zachariades. With this the rebels withdrew into Albania, and on October 16, 1949 the rebel radio conceded defeat, announcing the cessation of operations "to carry on the fight by other means." [34] It is noteworthy, in light of later events in Viet Nam and elsewhere, that the limited war in Greece did not end at a conference table. It simply petered out.

Since this is a study of the political aspects of limited war no attempt has been made to give a detailed account of military events. However, the Symmorito-Polemo of Greece was a tragic war from every human aspect. It was literally a case of Greek meeting Greek. There was no part of the peninsula or archipelago which did not suffer the ravages of this internecine conflict. As the guerrilla struggle continued there were times in 1947 and 1948 when the rebel forces controlled most of the mainland of Greece, or at least had made the country insecure.[35]

An eyewitness British observer calculated that in the period December 1944–September 1949 158,000 people had been killed — all Greeks. Eleven thousand men and women had fled the country. A tenth of the population had been displaced. Most horrifying of all, 25,000 children had been abducted by the guerrillas to the Communist sanctuaries north of the Greek frontier.[36] By the Spring of 1949 it was officially estimated that 10 per cent of the Greek population had become refugees, totaling 700,000.[37] However, this was only the number of those refugees receiving relief. The United Nations' fourth UNSCOB report estimated the full total of refugees to be as much as a million in January 1949.[38] Within Greece itself there were over 300,000 refugee children from the northern provinces settled in so-called child towns. This all too brief account of the human suffering endured in the Greek Civil War can best end with the following vignette:

"In the 'child town' in the village of Agria, near Volos, there was a photograph of four of the children on a seesaw, two at either end. The father of one pair had killed the father of the other; in revenge the grandfather of the orphans had killed the murderer." [39]

As usual in this type of limited war characterized by guerrilla activity and supplied from external Communist sanctuaries — the typical "war of national liberation" — the ratio of Communist partisans against which regular forces were pitted was exceedingly small. It has been estimated that the total of active Communist guerrillas taking part in the Symmorito-Polemo was not more than 25,000 men. Against these partisans stood a Greek regular army of 130,-

ooo men, augmented by 100 National Defense Corps battalions, plus the Royal Hellenic Navy and Air Force, a total of 265,000 men.

7.

Of lessons to be learned from the U.S. participation in the Civil War in Greece, at least four stand out.* Of these, the two most salient merit quotation in full:

> Plurality of command does not work. Although this seems basic, even so soon after World War II as 1947, this was attempted in Greece, both in the diplomatic field and in the military. There must be a single U.S. diplomatic representative to the host Government and there must be a single U.S. military commander who is responsible to him. In the situation in Greece, the former was not achieved until 1948 and the latter was not achieved until 1950, after the fighting was over.

As for the U.S. military Chief of Mission, he must indeed be an Admirable Crichton — the "parfit gentle knight":

> The Chief of Mission will succeed or fail, to a very great degree, depending upon his personality. That he is a capable Commander is not enough; he will actually command very few people. In addition to being a capable Commander, he must have many strings to his bow. He must be able to win the confidence and trust not only of the U.S. military, but of the U.S. Department of State and the U.S. diplomatic

---

* The scholarly study entitled "U.S. Military Participation in the Counterinsurgency Operation in Greece, 1947–1949" has listed a total of 30 "lessons to be learned."

Some of the thirty recommendations are in great detail. All are common sense; viz:

"28. Special attention must be paid to the traditional eating and food preparation habits of the host country. Taking this into consideration will often prevent much waste of food which will not be eaten. In Greece the recognition of the Greeks' preference for mutton over beef resulted in a saving of over thirty cents per pound."

representatives in the field. He must be able to win the acceptance and support of the host country military hierarchy and of its principal governmental officials. He must win the support of the third country officials who may be in the country, and he must be able to inspire respect and win the confidence of the military units and civilian population of the nation he is sent to advise. He must understand and be able to use effectively every method known in winning the support and confidence of these varied groups, from harsh determined action to the much more subtle shades of inter-personal relations.

And finally, on the host country side, "a single military officer of the country must be given complete authority to fight the counterinsurgent war free from petty political interference.

"The host government must support the counterinsurgent war if maximum results are to be obtained. If the politicians cannot be persuaded to support the war, they must at least be persuaded to refrain from interfering and making speeches and comments which have an adverse effect on the prosecution of the war." [40]

As indicated early in this chapter, the civil war in Greece was a war in which the main protagonists used substitute forces, or what this writer is fond of calling surrogate forces. On the Communist side, the pawns in the game were for the large part authentic Greeks. Greeks though they might have been, they were also authentic Communists. In addition, there were surrogate forces in Albania, Yugoslavia, and Bulgaria, at least to the extent of supplying training and logistic support.

On the American side, the chosen instrument was the Greek trooper. With increasing U.S. logistical support it finally came to the point that "during the Greek civil war, many a Greek soldier discovered that the only Greek thing about him was himself." [41] From the American point of view, the hero of the piece was a surrogate soldier. We shall find elsewhere in our studies of limited war in the second half of the century that one of the characteristics of these conflicts is the art of getting someone else to do the fighting.

It was in Greece that the United States first began to deploy foreign aid, both military and economic, to achieve political objectives. So successful has been the use of aid in the implementation of national foreign policies that it is now almost unbelievable to recall that, in 1948, Molotov walked out of the Paris Conference which considered the Marshall Plan and thus gave up an unheard-of opportunity for joining it and sabotaging European recovery from within. The true test of the efficacy of the U.S. foreign aid program, which started in the Greek Civil War, can be found in the fact that both the Communist great powers, the Soviet Union and China, have since followed our example and to a massive degree.

The Greek Civil War was one of the testing grounds of the United Nations in its obligation to maintain international peace. The United Nations had scarcely been formed, and organized the Security Council, when the Greek Government on December 3, 1946 lodged its complaint of intervention by the Communist countries to the north. Although the United Nations perhaps did not play a definitive role in bringing the conflict in Greece to a close; nevertheless, the reports of the Security Council Investigating Commission and the General Assembly's Balkan Committee unmistakably pointed the finger of guilt at the Communist powers; and world public opinion, thanks to these reports of the United Nations, was left in no ambiguity as to what the Communists were up to. The United Nations, as we shall see later, has been much involved, either in the center or on the periphery, in limited war. The Symmorito-Polemo in Greece was merely the first of a long series.

Finally, the Greek experience commenced the slow, laborious and difficult process which was the evolution of the Country Team — the coordination of the efforts of various departments and agencies of the U.S. Government working abroad as a symphonic unit under the direction of the Ambassador. We shall comment later on the developing of this concept.

Thus the Symmorito-Polemo ended in a basic strategic defeat of the Communist forces. It witnessed the commencement of historic processes of reaction by the Free World to Communist aggression, which later reappeared in other limited wars which are subject to our study. Although the Soviet strategic thrust toward the Mediterranean was checked, it was not long before the Communists moved again. This time their push was on the opposite side of the world, seeking once more dominion in the sea. This time the thrust was in Korea.

CHAPTER IV

The War in Korea, 1950–1953

1.

"THIS TIME the thrust was in Korea." Once more Communist power sought a strategic objective and once more the means used to a wider end was limited war.

After his repulse in the Greek Civil War and the advent of the Truman Doctrine and the Marshall Plan, Stalin made one final attempt in Europe to check the rise of Free World power which his own actions had evoked. This was the blockade of Berlin, which was successfully surmounted by the airlift from April 1, 1948, to September 30, 1949. In the same year the balance of power began to shift in the Far East. Mao Tse-tung and his Communist forces defeated the armies of Chiang Kai-shek and drove the remnants of the Nationalist Government and Army to refuge on Taiwan.

If Stalin's eyes now ranged toward the Western Pacific he had ample evidence from Russian history of interest in that area.

For centuries Korea has been regarded either as "a dagger pointed at the heart of Japan" or as a bridge by which the Pacific Powers might thrust into North China, Manchuria and the Maritime Provinces of Siberia. In the days of the Ming Dynasty and the great Japanese Shogun, Hideyoshi, Korea was the battleground of contending forces seeking dominance of the Yellow Sea and the Sea of Japan.* Later, in the failing days of the Kingdom of Korea, when Chinese suzerain power was challenged both by Russia and Japan, and Korea had briefly been occupied by Japan in the Sino-Japanese War of 1894–1895, the significant 38th parallel was proposed in 1896 by General Yamagata Aritomo as the line of demarcation between imperial Russian and Japanese power.[2] The Russo-Japanese War of 1904 ended all that, and Chosen, the "Land of Morning Calm," entered into the calm of mourning. Only a scant handful of patriots in exile, such as Syngman Rhee, kept alive the flickering hope of freedom for Korea.

Although a war aim was declared at the Cairo Conference in 1943 that Korea should eventually be independent, nothing was actually said at the Yalta Conference in the Top Secret document entitled "Terms for the Entry of the Soviet Union into the War against Japan." [3] However, among the conditions which Stalin attached for his entry into World War II there was implicitly a restoration of former Russian imperial power in Northeast Asia.[4] In consequence it seemed merely as if history were repeating itself when, two days before the collapse of Japan, on August 12, 1945, 100,000 Soviet troops under General Chistiakov crossed the Siberian border into North Korea.[5] At the suggestion of the U.S. War Department, ratified by the Joint Chiefs of Staff,[6] once more the fateful line of the 38th parallel marked the division between Soviet and U.S. occupying forces, based on Japan. American troops entered South Korea on September 8.

At the meeting of Foreign Ministers in Moscow in 1945 it was agreed to establish a Joint (U.S. — U.S.S.R.) Commission to make recommendations for a single free government

---

* Hideyoshi invaded Korea in 1592 and 1597; the *Nunobiki* or mound of pickled noses and ears of fallen Koreans still stands in his city of Kyoto as a grisly monument. The Japanese were destroyed at sea by the first iron-clads used in naval warfare under the Korean Admiral, Yi Sun-sin; but in general they were victorious on land in the peninsula. Hideyoshi's ambition was the conquest of China. He died in September 1598.[1] The ambition died later.

in Korea.* Meanwhile, there would be a five-year, Four Power Trusteeship over that divided country. However, the Russians were busily and successfully organizing a satellite state in North Korea and had no intention whatever of living up to the Moscow Agreement.[7] In 1947, therefore, the United States took the Korean matter to the United Nations and secured a resolution from the General Assembly calling for nationwide elections to be held in the spring of 1948. These elections were to be observed by a nine-member U.N. Commission — the first direct popular elections in 4000 years of Korean history. As could have been expected, the Soviet Union refused to allow the Commission north of the 38th parallel where its own arrangements for a "Democratic People's Republic of Korea" were well advanced. Elections were, however, held in South Korea, a National Assembly was seated and it in turn named Syngman Rhee as President of the Republic of Korea.[8] In the North the Communists proclaimed the Democratic People's Republic of Korea with "Kim Il Sung" as Prime Minister.

Kim, who also fought as a guerrilla leader under the name of Kim Sung Chu, was an alumnus of a school of banditry in Manchuria which operated against the Japanese before World War II. Some authorities have cast doubt upon his authenticity as the real Kim Il Sung.[9] He certainly fought as a captain in the Red Army at Stalingrad and was thoroughly a Russo-Red. This was typical of other North Korean leaders, such as Choe Young Gun, another guerrilla leader, Ho Kai, Secretary of the North Korean Labor Party (forced to commit suicide in 1952) and Nam Il, presently Deputy Prime Minister and the North Korean negotiator at Panmunjom; Koreans by face

---

* It is perhaps germane to this over-all study of limited war to note that in September 1947 the Soviet delegation in the Joint Commission made the first proposal for the "withdrawal of foreign forces" (U.S. and U.S.S.R. in Korea) — a theme which was central in subsequent confrontations, namely the Geneva Conference of 1954, the Geneva Conference of 1962, the Taiwan Straits crisis of 1958, and now the main pitch of Hanoi in the current Viet Nam war.

and race, they began life as Soviet citizens, born and reared in the Korean minority in the U.S.S.R. which had been moved in the 1930's from Siberia to the Kazakhstan-Uzbekistan area. Thus, having created a Soviet satellite government in North Korea staffed with dedicated Communists who were Koreans, either citizens of the Soviet Union, veterans of the Soviet Army, or recent soldiers for Mao Tse-tung, buttressed in turn by Soviet advisers, Stalin thought his grasp on North Korea so secure that he could now remove Russian troops. In consequence, by the end of 1948 with great ostentation his soldiers had evacuated Korea. They left behind them a well-trained and well-equipped North Korean People's Army for which the armed forces of South Korea were certainly no match.[10]

By June 1949 the United States had followed suit by withdrawing its 50,000 troops from South Korea. However, because of fear that Syngman Rhee might act on his often-repeated threat to take North Korea by force, the United States Korean Military Advisory Group (one of the first of our later ubiquitous MAAGS) administered an aid program for the ROK Army which excluded air, armor, or heavy artillery. Coincidental with this policy decision, the U.S. Defense Department made no secret of its military opinion that Korea was outside the defense perimeter of the United States in East Asia; an opinion which was given worldwide publicity on January 12, 1950, when stated by the Secretary of State, Dean Acheson, in a speech at the National Press Club in Washington.

2.

Under these circumstances it was not difficult for Stalin to reach the conclusion that now was the time to achieve Russia's purpose that had been frustrated by the Japanese in Korea at the beginning of the century. Stalin had been repulsed in his strategic thrust to the Mediterranean through the proxy conflict of the Greek Civil War, and the airlift had outdone him at Berlin. Now, persuaded by the Americans' own statements that they would not react, possessed of a docile and willing satellite at Pyongyang, and commanding a vast battle-trained Soviet military machine with ample stocks of weapons to equip soldiers, there seemed indeed no reason from the Kremlin's point of view not to undertake this strategic stab through the peninsula of Korea which might eventually neutralize and ultimately capture Japan for Communism. If successful, the thrust could remove American power from the Western Pacific. As to whether the secular conflict between Russia and China would resume, that was a matter for the future. At the moment China was weak. Mao Tse-tung was a newly recruited ally and his ambitions were turned elsewhere, toward the conquest of Taiwan and the invasion of Tibet. Furthermore, in 1949 Stalin had acquired his own atomic bomb.

The instrument of Stalin's strategic thrust was the North Korean striking force under General Chai Ung Chai. It was a tough, well-trained, superbly equipped army, numbering 90,000 men or two-thirds of the total North Korean Army's strength of 135,000, not counting the border constabulary. Unlike the South Koreans, the invaders from the North had Russian tanks, heavy artillery, and some aircraft. The South Korean Army totaled 143,000, of which 45,000 were National Police and 33,000 service and staff personnel, leaving only 65,000 fighting men on the line.[11]

Although on paper the forces seemed evenly matched, in reality the North Koreans were a tempered sword against the bamboo staves of the ROK. The invasion began on Sunday, the 25th of June, 1950.

The military story has been so frequently recounted that only the briefest summary is necessary. The triumphant North Korean forces marched quickly to the banks of the

River Han, overran Seoul, and pushed on toward Pusan, the port at the southern extremity of the peninsula. The United States first called upon only naval and air forces to deploy. The Supreme Commander in the Far East, General Mac-Arthur, was ordered to take action by air and naval forces to prevent the Inchon-Kimpo-Seoul areas from falling into unfriendly hands. At the same time the Seventh Fleet was deployed to the Formosa Strait to prevent either the Chinese Communists from invading Taiwan or the forces of Chiang Kai-shek from landing on the mainland. Desperate resistance by the ROK Army and a handful of U.S. troops falling back from Seoul, reinforced from Japan, at last stabilized a precarious front on the Pusan perimeter.

However, while the Communists were winning military victories with giant strides in Korea, they were busily losing the war on the diplomatic front, by one of the most gigantic blunders which Soviet diplomacy has displayed in the near half-century of the Soviet Union's existence.

On the day of the North Korean attack that Sunday, June 25, the United States asked the United Nations Secretary General, Trygve Lie, to convene the Security Council, which met at 2 P.M. New York time. Now, the U.S.S.R. had boycotted the Security Council since January on the pretext that it would not sit at the same table with the representative of Nationalist China. In consequence, when the time came to take the vote on U.N. participation in the war against aggression in Korea, Jacob Malik, the Soviet delegate, was nowhere to be seen and the famous Russian veto remained locked in his diplomatic briefcase.

The Security Council lost no time in calling for a ceasefire and withdrawal of the North Korean forces beyond the 38th parallel. Four days later in a historic resolution, the Council recommended "that the members of the United Nations furnish such assistance to the Republic of Korea as may be necessary to repel the armed attack and to restore international peace and security in the area." On July 7 the Council authorized a unified United Nations Command and asked the United States to appoint that Commander. It was not until August that the U.S.S.R. belatedly returned to the Council when its month's rotation of the Presidency was due. It was then considerably too late to claim that all acts taken in the absence of the Soviet delegate were "illegal." In fact by that time sixteen nations had pledged contingents to the U.N. forces in Korea under their American Commander.

Here again we find in our study of limited war that curious characteristic — at least of latter-twentieth-century limited war — the use of surrogate soldiers. In the North Korean Army Stalin had his combatants by proxy, while the United States leaned on a frailer reed in the ROK Army. The most gigantic proxy, however, was the United Nations Command. In the legal sense it was a proxy working for the American side since the sixteen nations committed to the defense of South Korea were technically agents of the U.N. In another sense, however, the Americans were the proxy combatants of the United Nations, since the Command and the major bulk of the modern fighting forces were American. Presently the war would see an interjection of new and even more sinister surrogate soldiers in the form of Chinese "volunteers."

After the last-ditch defense of Pusan the fortunes of war changed. General MacArthur executed his brilliant landing at Inchon; the ruined city of Seoul was liberated and the now triumphant U.N. forces, made up principally of South Korean and American troops, ably served by U.S. naval and air power on either coast, moved north.

3.

Communist China began to stir. On September 30 Chou En-lai announced publicly that China would not "supinely tolerate" seeing Korea "invaded by the imperialists." On

October 1 the Supreme Commander, General MacArthur, broadcast an ultimatum to North Korea demanding unconditional surrender. It was on that night that Chou En-lai summoned the Indian Ambassador, K. M. Panikkar, to a midnight conference in Peking and told him that if U.S. troops invaded North Korea, China would enter the war. This signal was at once flashed to New Delhi and thence to Washington, where President Truman evaluated it in light of his belief that if in fact Ambassador Panikkar was not operating on the Communist side of the street he at least was driving to the left.[12]

Also on October 1 units of the ROK Army crossed the 38th parallel. It was not until a week later, on October 7, that the Eighth Army followed suit.

October 7 is a date to remember. In addition to the American decision to cross the historic parallel it was on October 7 that the United Nations General Assembly passed its resolution authorizing U.N. action in North Korea. By coincidence, perhaps, October 7 also marked the day when the armies of Red China commenced their invasion of Tibet.[13] It was ironical that India, which had been working so strenuously on behalf of the Communist Powers, should now feel the brunt of Chinese Communist aggression against the buffer state which warded its Himalayan frontier.

We now come to a monumental miscalculation in military and political intelligence.

On October 15, meeting with President Truman on Wake Island, General MacArthur told the President, "I believe that formal resistance will end throughout North Korea by Thanksgiving." As for the possibility of Chinese Communist intervention, he told the President there was "very little. Had they interfered in the first or second months it would have been decisive. We are no longer fearful of their intervention." [14]

On the following day the first of 180,000 Chinese troops

began crossing the Yalu River into North Korea, commanded by General Lin Piao, who later as Minister of Defense of Communist China enunciated the Manifesto of September 2, 1965, drawing up Mao Tse-tung's monstrous blueprint for "wars of national liberation." Lin Piao commanded the Fourth Field Army. Its skillful deployment, the troops marching at night and lying up in the daytime in caves or camouflaged revetments to prevent air intelligence discovery, permitted a vast army secretly to install itself in North Korea, while the G–2 of General MacArthur continued to report the Chinese units as battalions instead of actual divisions.

The rest of the story is tragically brief. The U.N. forces continued their advance toward the Yalu. Pyongyang, the capital of North Korea, still held out but was occupied on October 19–21.* While the Eighth Army under General Walker, the Tenth Corps under General Almond, and the ROK divisions marched to the Yalu, the secret forces of General Lin Piao's "volunteers" uncoiled like a triggered spring. On October 25 the Chinese Communist 124th Division struck the ROK 3rd Division at Sudong, and the ROK 7th Division, which had reached the Yalu, was trapped and destroyed. The ROK Second Corps collapsed and took to flight by November 1; and on November 6 General Mac-Arthur's special communiqué announced that a "new war" had begun.[15]

There now ensued a curious lull in the fighting as the Chinese Communist command broke off action until November 26. Undoubtedly Peking was assessing the situation, studying the auspices, marking up the intricate arithmetic which goes into the assessment of a "calculated risk." As one

* A curious monograph resulted from the brief American occupation of Pyongyang. Hastily the Department of State sent a group of learned researchers to interview the captured Communist bureaucrats in Pyongyang. The results of this rapid but thorough study are incorporated in a State Department publication aptly entitled *North Korea: A Case Study in the Techniques of Takeover*.

authority has commented, "While China crossed the Yalu on October 15th, she did not cross the Rubicon until November 26th." [16]

Before undertaking the more difficult and speculative task of assaying China's reasons for entering the Korean War, it is simpler and more easily documented to summarize the United States' reasons for crossing the 38th parallel. In the first place, the United States had won a remarkable and dramatic victory at Inchon. The forces of the U.N. Command restored the capital of Seoul to the Korean Government and the broken North Korean Army in disheveled retreat presented no military obstacle to the investment of Pyongyang and, seemingly, the reunification of all Korea from Pusan to the Manchurian-Siberian frontier. This indeed was the mandate of the United Nations and it was the unfailing goal of Syngman Rhee. However, despite the apparent military defeat of North Korea, no signal came from its regime of any surrender or even willingness to negotiate or terminate the hostilities. Therefore, why not press on to victory? And, since it is deeply ingrained in the American character to fight for victory when the United States becomes involved in war, surely so astute a politician as President Truman was not oblivious of the fact that victory would help him in the November elections.

The reasons for China's entry into the war are less easy of assessment but nevertheless clear. It should be noted at this point that the objectives of the arch-conspirator, Stalin, remained unchanged. The Soviet Union continued to supply the sinews of war to its proxy protagonists; only now the surrogate soldiers had changed. They were no longer the beaten North Korean Army, but the battle-tested and ant-like masses of the Chinese Fourth Field Army disguised under the thin veneer of "volunteers."

On the basis of the evidence available it seems probable

that Communist China had not participated in planning the attack which Stalin launched on the 25th of June 1950 through his North Korean puppets. Peking, in fact, had shown a scarcely disdainful interest in the regime at Pyongyang, which it tacitly acknowledged as a Soviet satellite. Furthermore, Peking had enough problems on its mind without concerning itself with developments in North Korea. The entire thrust of Mao's military preparations was toward the south and west. The Third Field Army was massing for the contemplated amphibious attack on Taiwan and armies in Szechuan were preparing for the invasion of Tibet. The repositioning of the Fourth Field Army into Manchuria seemed at first merely a precautionary move to establish a strategic reserve in an area vital to Chinese security.

However, the collapse of North Korea after the Inchon landing evoked a defensive response. Korea might be "a dagger pointed at the heart of Japan" but it is also a bridge to Manchuria and North China, as Hideyoshi had shown in the time of the Ming Emperors, and the Japanese later had proved in the wars with China and Russia in 1894–95 and 1904–05. Fundamental to the decision to enter the war in Korea was the question of Japan. Both the Communist powers, the U.S.S.R. and Communist China, feared an emergent alliance between the United States and Japan which would ensure dominance of the Western Pacific. If, however, in Korea American power could be blunted and possibly destroyed Japan might be kept free of such an association with the leading power of the non-Communist world. Japan might ultimately in the event of a Communist takeover in Korea enter the camp of Moscow and Peking.

There is little doubt, however, that Mao Tse-tung was aware of Stalin's intention to invade South Korea by his surrogate North Korean forces. In fact, two Chicom Divisions composed of Koreans from the million and a half minority in Manchuria who provided shock troops for the taking of Mukden from the Chinese Nationalists were sent to North Korea in late 1949 and early 1950 to be used as cadres for the shock divisions in the aggression of June 25, 1950. We know also from a Soviet defector from the Russian Embassy in Tokyo that he had carried a personal message from Stalin to Mao Tse-tung in the early autumn of 1950 urging Chinese Communist intervention in North Korea and promising Soviet material support. The defector added that there were telephone conversations subsequently between Mao and Stalin on this subject.

However, the evidence is persuasive that Communist China entered the war in Korea of its own volition and not as the result of a *dikat* from Stalin. It was an Asian decision reached for Asian reasons or, as one authority has put it, "the final decision to fight appears to have been basically a Chinese decision, conditioned by Russian advice and encouraged by Russian support." [17]

At this point it is useful to consider how the United States assessed the potential Chinese Communist intention to enter the war; and how Peking misinterpreted the intent of the United States to limit the war.

President Truman and his diplomatic and military advisers had early understood the danger of possible Chinese intervention and the risk that the Korean War could escalate into World War III with the Soviet Union and Communist China as formidable adversaries. As early as October 9 President Truman approved a directive to General MacArthur "in light of the possible intervention of Chinese Communist forces in North Korea."

The President added:

Hereafter in the event of the open or covert employment anywhere in Korea of major Chinese Communist units, without prior announcement, you should continue the action as long as, in your judgment, action by forces now under your control offers a reasonable chance of success. In any case you will obtain authorization from Washington prior to taking any military action against objectives in Chinese territory. [18]

Later General Marshall, as Secretary of Defense, and the Joint Chiefs of Staff were emphatic in the belief that "we should not get ourselves involved either individually or with the United Nations in a general war with China." Secretary Acheson said, "We had banked our entire foreign policy on the idea of keeping Russia contained, and we had succeeded in repulsing her attempts to break out. If we allowed the Russians now to trap us inside their perimeter, however, we would run the risk of being sucked into a bottomless pit." [19] As the Chairman of the Joint Chiefs, General Omar Bradley, put it in the meeting of the National Security Council with President Truman on November 28, 1950, "We should be in the wrong war, at the wrong place, at the wrong time, and with the wrong enemy." [20]

If Washington was clear in its resolve that the Korean War should not escalate into World War III, it was less clear how victory could be denied the Chinese Communists. Starting on November 26, the divisions of the Fourth Field Army, now numbering thirty, commenced their victorious drive south — the Chonchong defeat of General MacArthur. They were not checked until Seoul had once more fallen into Communist hands and the U.N. defense perimeter was formed south of the capital city.

The cries of General MacArthur for widening the war became more shrill. On March 24 he issued a statement advocating extending the war to mainland China.[21] In a letter to Representative Joseph Martin, which the latter read to the House of Representatives on April 5, 1951, MacArthur wrote "as you point out, we must win. There is no substitute for

victory." Martin's speech of February 12 in which he said,
"If we are not in Korea to win, then this Administration
should be indicted for the murder of thousands of American
boys" was certainly not calculated to endear either him or
MacArthur, his endorser, to the Administration. On April
10, at one o'clock in the morning, President Truman announced that General MacArthur had been relieved of his
command in the Far East. President Truman in a broadcast to the nation said, "In the simplest terms, what we are
doing in Korea is this: we are trying to prevent World War
III. So far, by fighting a limited war in Korea, we have prevented aggression from succeeding and bringing on a general
war." [22]

As for the great World War II Commander in the Pacific,
General MacArthur clearly never understood the true nature
of limited war. In his testimony before the Senate Armed
Services and Foreign Relations Committees in May and
June 1951, he said that limited war in Korea had "intro-
duce[d] a new concept into military operations — the concept of appeasement, the concept that when you use force
you can limit that force . . . I think that introduces into the
military sphere a political control such as I have never known
in my life or have ever studied . . ." [23]

4.

Under the new management of the war in Korea, with
General Ridgway as Supreme Commander Far East and General Van Fleet, Commander of U.N. Forces in Korea, the
Eighth Army inflicted great losses on the Communist enemy
and beyond doubt they were ready for destruction by the
middle of June 1951. In one year of war 500,000 casualties
had been suffered by the North Korean Army and it was vir-
tually eliminated as a fighting force. In only eight months of

conflict the Chinese Communists had lost an estimated half a million men. It was therefore not surprising that on June 23 the Soviet Delegate to the United Nations, Jacob Malik, in a U.N. radio broadcast suggested a cease-fire and armistice "providing for mutual withdrawal of forces from the 38th parallel." Two days later the Peking newspaper, *People's Daily*, endorsed the proposal. Ambassador Kirk in Moscow was told by Foreign Minister Gromyko that the armistice would be military only. On June 30, General Ridgway broadcast a message to the Commander in Chief of the Communist Forces in Korea proposing talks. On the following night, Kim Il Sung and the Chinese Communist General, Peng Teh-huai, agreed to the initial meeting at Kaesong.[24] *

This first meeting at Kaesong, July 10 to August 23, was a snarling match in which both sides traded invective. It broke off when the Communists trumped up a charge of "American bombing of Kaesong" as a pretext to terminate the talks. However, continuing U.N. advances once more brought the Communists back to the conference table by the second week in October, this time meeting at Panmunjom, a hamlet of four houses situated between Munsan and Kaesong. The talks dragged on and the war reached a bloody stalemate roughly along the lines of the fatal and fateful 38th parallel.[25]

In November 1952, General Eisenhower was elected President of the United States. He noted that at that time "American casualties had reached a total of 21,000 killed, 91,000 wounded and 13,000 missing; making this the fourth

* In the clearer vision of hindsight it seems probable that at this point the United States made its second great misjudgment of the Korean War, following MacArthur's classic miscalculation of the enemy's resources when the Chinese crossed the Yalu. At the time armistice talks began the Chinese were in a reversed situation so far as their forces in Korea were concerned: they were not victors but vanquished. Yet the war was protracted another two years for the same ultimate result at a high cost in American and Asian lives and economic strength.

most costly conflict in United States history, ranking only behind the Civil War and the two World Wars."[26] The President-elect made a personal visit to Korea, arriving on December 2, 1952. He said, "My conclusion as I left Korea was that we could not stand forever on a static front and continue to accept casualties without any visible results. Small attacks on small hills would not end this war."[27] In the new President's first inaugural address he announced that the Seventh Fleet would no longer patrol the waters between Formosa and the Chinese mainland to prevent an attack on Taiwan, and also to insure that island would not be used as a base of operations against the Chinese Communist mainland. Said the President, "There is no longer any logic or sense in a condition that required the United States Navy to assume defensive responsibilities on behalf of the Chinese Communists."[28]

President Eisenhower's memoirs state, "Finally, to keep the attack from becoming overly costly, it was clear that we would have to use atomic weapons." He describes diplomatic initiatives to drop hints at Panmunjom, New Delhi and elsewhere that the United States was getting impatient and intended to move incisively without inhibition in its use of weapons unless an armistice could be achieved. The President claims that very shortly thereafter the Communists began to change their attitude in the conversations at Panmunjom.[29]

However, a perhaps more decisive event was the death on March 5, 1953 of Joseph Stalin.

In any case, on March 28, 1953, Kim Il Sung and General Peng replied to General Clark's offer of February 22 for an exchange of sick and wounded prisoners, accepting the offer and proposing an armistice. The first exchange of sick and wounded — "Operation Little Switch" — was agreed to on April 11 and the exchange began on the 26th of that month.

A much bigger exchange of prisoners, "Operation Big Switch," began three months later.[30] *

By June 8, 1953, agreement had been reached at Panmunjom on the question of whether war prisoners should be compulsively repatriated or given their choice on where to go, and an armistice agreement was on the point of signature. It was on the night of June 17–18 that the desperate and intransigent President of the Republic of Korea, Syngman Rhee, who was adamantly opposed to an armistice, sabotaged the Panmunjom talks by releasing 25,000 North Korean prisoners of war who were instantly absorbed into the population, refusing repatriation to the north. As Rhee had anticipated, the Chinese Communists broke off the armistice talks in consequence. There ensued a difficult month of negotiations to placate the furious President of the Republic of Korea, but finally the Assistant Secretary of State for Far Eastern Affairs, Walter Robertson, persuaded Syngman Rhee to agree to an armistice in return for many promises of American support and aid. The President of Korea's reluctant acquiescence was incorporated in an agreement signed July 11, 1953.[32] On July 27, 1953, the armistice agreement was signed at Panmunjom.

Although the Berlin meeting of Foreign Ministers in January–February 1954 agreed that a final political settlement on Korea should also occupy the Geneva Conference which met on Indochina April 26, the latter question was paramount and the dialogues on Korea, although eloquent, were fruitless. Here again a military armistice has been confirmed by the pressures of the balance of power into an uneasy *de facto* peace without a treaty of peace having been negotiated. A

---

* It is interesting, in view of President Eisenhower's assertion that the threat of possible use of atomic weapons influenced the Communists to come to the armistice table, that actually Chou En-lai's response which led to "Little Switch" and "Big Switch" came on March 28, 1953, almost two months before Secretary Dulles visited New Delhi.[31]

similar uncertain end to a bitter war had been reached in the conflict between Israel and the Arabs.

5.

In conclusion it can be said that Korea was the archetype of limited war.

In the first place, the war was limited as to its theater. It was restricted to the embattled peninsula of Korea itself. A corollary of this fact was that it was a war of sanctuaries. Inhibitions imposed by both sides on themselves prevented the spread of war beyond the peninsula although support of the war on both sides was exterior. This gave rise to the anomalous situation of the Manchurian sanctuary that was used as a staging ground for Chinese "volunteer" troops and the Siberian sanctuary where Soviet massive aid in equipment and supplies was mobilized. There was also the sanctuary of North China itself, vulnerable at any time to the destructive power of the American Air Force.

However, on the other side there were the United States sanctuaries in Japan. No Soviet bombing planes sought out the American concentration of troops and matériel in ports such as Fukuoka and Nagasaki, nor the great arsenals and repair shops on Honshu. There was also a sanctuary at sea. No Soviet or Chinese Communist submarines sought to impede the unfettered use of the narrow seas by the U.S. Seventh Fleet. Only in Korean territorial waters, particularly at Wonsan, was Russia's superiority in mining technique put to effective use. And finally, the greatest U.S. sanctuary was within Korea itself. There were no Communist air raids on the highly vulnerable ports, or the unprotected supply centers in the rear, and — except for "Washing Machine Charlie" type of nuisance raids — none on our front lines. The air battle was for air supremacy over North Korea.

There was a refusal by both the U.S. and U.S.S.R. to widen

the war either territorially or strategically to escalate to World War III. Thus, on the American side the policy was steadfastly to refuse extending the conflict to mainland China, to involve Taiwan, or directly to involve the U.S.S.R. The Soviet Union for its part, the only Communist power capable of reaching the United States in its heartland, was discreetly diffident. Communist China was neither discreet nor diffident, but lacked the economic and military potential to fill its polemics with power.

There was limitation of the use of weapons in this limited war. Despite President Eisenhower's animadversions on the possibility of using the nuclear weapon, it was not used. For that matter, neither did the Russians use the atomic bomb which they had acquired by 1949. As for the Communist Chinese, it seems that they considered the possibility of atomic retaliation and dismissed it as being both improbable and, in any event, not compelling in the case of China. As the Acting Chief of Staff, General Nieh Yen-jung, remarked to Indian Ambassador Panikkar, atomic attacks might "kill a few million people," but "after all, China lives on the farms. What can atom bombs do there?"[33]

As indicated previously, the war in Korea was marked by the massive use of surrogate forces. Both sides used the hapless Koreans as their soldiers by proxy. The Soviet Union also used Chinese "volunteers" to achieve its purpose while the United States through the United Nations had the proxy of fifteen other nations. However, for the first time in history there was massive direct confrontation of American versus Chinese troops. This was no proxy.

And finally, the Korean War was limited by the fact that both sides reduced their objectives from taking all of the peninsula to settling for a stalemate approximating the old Russo-Japanese line of the balance of power, the 38th parallel.

The cost was great. In terms of human life, according to

U.S. estimates, the Chinese Communists had casualties of 900,000 dead and wounded while the North Koreans lost 520,000 dead and wounded. On the United Nations side, the South Koreans suffered the most in the total casualties of 150,000 dead and 250,000 wounded. The American battle losses went higher than at the time of President Eisenhower's election, totaling 33,629 dead and 103,284 wounded.* Of the other U.N. allies no single nation lost more than 1,000 dead.[34]

The physical losses in Korea were vast. Both capitals, Seoul and Pyongyang, were practically destroyed. There can be no measurement for the other losses in terms of human suffering and the division of a people against itself.

Another loss from the aspect of the Free World was the gain in prestige and "face" of Communist China, which had challenged the world's greatest power in battle. On the other hand, Communist China also lost, because the optimum moment for the invasion of Taiwan, for which it was poised for attack in 1950, was irrevocably let slip. At no future time could Mao Tse-tung count on Nationalist power on Taiwan being so weak as it was at that fatal date when the military resources of Communist China were diverted to the North Korean adventure.

On the positive side of the ledger, the Free World gains far exceeded its losses. In the first place, Stalin's historic Russian thrust into Korea was broken by the United States at Inchon and the Yalu. Thenceforth the onus was placed on Chinese Communist shoulders. And China's historic thrust into Korea was blunted and was on the point of being broken, when armistice talks produced a stalemate and eventual settlement at the 38th parallel. In the broad sweep of

---

* The author remembers the silent breakfast he shared in the mess of the 7th Regiment, 7th Division, on the MLR (Main Line of Resistance) in 1952 when it was learned that during the night a probing patrol had been wiped out and seats at table would be forever empty. This was the day when he was given the satisfaction of firing a 105 mm. gun-howitzer at the Communist Chinese.

strategy the main Communist war aim was made impossible of achievement: Japan was left independent and an ally of the United States; the Free World was still dominant in the Western Pacific.

The United Nations had fought its first war and come through to a peaceful settlement. The United Nations was new in business but had proved its utility against Communist aggression three times in the first five years of its existence: at Azerbaijan, in the Greek Civil War, and now in Korea. In fact if any conclusion is valid in this study of limited war it is that the United Nations will be involved, hopefully to good effect, in most of them.

Most important of all from the consideration of the world balance of power, the outward thrust of Communism toward the seas had once more decisively been thwarted — on one side of the globe in the Aegean and Mediterranean seas and now in Asian waters in the Yellow Sea and the Sea of Japan.

This was the last great confrontation of U.S. and Chinese Communist power until Viet Nam, with the exception of the episode in the Taiwan Straits in 1958. Other direct confrontations of U.S. and Soviet power were to ensue as at Berlin and in Cuba, but without leading to war. However, as pointed out at the beginning of this book, these were limited exercises in general war rather than general exercises in limited war.

Not all limited wars in the penultimate part of the twentieth century are of Communist origin, although the Communists are ever vigilant to seize on opportunities they may present. Such were three exercises in limited war in the Near East, staged on or near the Tri-Continental Position, the only link by land and sea between three Continents. These were the Arab-Israeli war of 1947–49, the Anglo-Israeli-French conspiracy at Sinai and Suez, in 1956, and the American landings in Lebanon two years thereafter.

CHAPTER V

Limited War for National Independence:
The Israeli-Arab War, 1947–1949

1.

WE NOW enter upon the study of three exercises in limited war which had no direct Communist connotation. These three episodes — the Israeli War for independence against the Arabs, the Israeli-Franco-British attack at Sinai and Suez, and the American landings in Lebanon — have one element of unity in that they all took place in the neuralgic area of the Middle East. In the sense of world strategy, these limited wars jeopardized the only tri-continental position on the globe. This is the land and sea crossroads between Europe, Africa and Asia which runs from the Bosporus along the Levant to Suez, linking Asia, Europe and Africa and, via the Persian Gulf and the Red Sea, the Indian Ocean and the further East.

This area of the world is the exchange point through which people, their belongings and, above all, their ideas, have transited throughout 5000 recorded years of history. In addition, in the era of hydrocarbon energy, it is the depository of the world's largest resource in oil. The birthplace of three world religions, the precepts of the Bible, Koran and Talmud signally failed to mitigate the fierce struggle between the Semitic cousins, Arab and Jew, which resulted from the birth of Israel.

To write of the war in Palestine is difficult because perhaps no limited war has awakened such violent emotions and has exerted such a worldwide tug on feeling as the bitter struggle between Arab and Jew which resulted in the establishment of the Jewish State of Israel. For the author the story is more easy and at the same time more difficult to tell because for two years he was totally involved as a minor participant in the diplomatic effort of the United States to see that justice was done, that the United Nations should be upheld, and that peace should eventually be restored to the tri-continental crossroad.

In the course of these two years of intimate connection with the war in Palestine the author had personal acquaintance of the main protagonists. On the Jewish side there was Dr. Chaim Weizmann, the elder statesman of the Zionist movement and the first President of Israel; Ben Gurion, with his halo of gray hair and face of an Old Testament prophet, the real architect of the state of Israel; Shertok (who changed his name later to Sharett), the Foreign Minister of Israel; Abba Eben, the brilliant representative of Israel at the United Nations and later Ambassador in Washington; Elishu Elath (then called Epstein), the Jewish expert on the Arabs, who was the first Ambassador of the Provisional Government of Israel in Washington; and Dr. Judah Magnes, President of the Hebrew University, who was not a Zionist and who had grave misgivings as to the ultimate prospects for the new Jewish State.

On the Arab side the author knew Faris el Khoury, the Prime Minister of Syria; Farid Zenneddin, the Ambassador of Syria to the United States; the Iraqi Foreign Minister, Jamali; the Secretary General of the Arab League, Abdul Razzam Pasha; Mahmoud Fawzi, the Foreign Minister of Egypt; and the Arab military leaders whom he knew after the war: General Naguib, Gamal Abdul Nasser, Hakim

Amer, and the Commander in Chief of the Lebanese forces and later President of Lebanon, General Fuad Chehab.

On the British side, in addition to the diplomatic contingent at the United Nations, there were Sir Michael Wright in the Foreign Office in London, Sir John Troutbeck, the British Minister for Middle Eastern Affairs stationed at Cairo, and the legendary Brigadier Clayton, the Oriental expert of the British diplomatic arm in the Near East, with his inevitable horsehair flywhisk, cross between swagger stick and scepter.

On the American side, as Special Assistant to Dean Rusk, who was then head of the Office of United Nations Affairs in the Department of State, the writer worked directly for him, Under Secretary of State Robert Lovett, and Secretary of State General George Marshall. As for the U.N. itself there was on needed occasion almost daily contact with Dr. Ralph Bunche, with the Secretary General, Trygve Lie, and, on the distant Island of Rhodes, with Count Folke Bernadotte, the United Nations Mediator, whom the author had known on a previous tour of duty in Sweden.

2.

The Palestine problem as between Arab and Jew has been vexed ever since the beginning of World War I. At that time the British, to gain advantage in the war against the Ottoman Empire, made seeming promises to the Arab leaders which were at sharp variance with a subsequent promise made in 1917 to the Jews of the world in the Balfour Declaration.

An exchange of letters in Arabic from July 14 to October 24, 1915, between the Sharif of Mecca, Hussein,* and Sir Henry McMahon, the British High Commissioner in Egypt,

---

* Later King of the Hejaz, father of King Abdullah of Jordan and King Feisal I of Iraq.

apparently promised to the Arabs the lands to the west of the "districts" (Wilayat) of Aleppo, Hama, Homs and Damascus.[1] In the next year the Sykes-Picot Agreement of 1916, which was later joined into by Imperial Russia, drew up zones of interest and influence in the Turkish Near East in early anticipation of the carving up of the Ottoman Empire. In these days of "sovereign equality" among the new nations, it is interesting to see that most of Western Anatolia was divided into an area of "Italian influence" and an outright "Italian Zone" while the Levant, including all of Syria and much of Turkey, was to be a French Zone abutting on a Russian area extending along the Black Sea. There was to be in the region of Iraq and Jordan an "Arab State under French influence" and also in Iraq, Saudi Arabia and Sinai an "Arab state under British guidance." In consequence the Allies' faces were red when in 1917 the Bolshevik Government published the Russian Foreign Office archives and the Arabs learned of this exercise in non-self-determination.[2]

However, a true bombshell for the Arabs was the Balfour Declaration of November 2, 1917, which as one authority has correctly stated "was carefully and deliberately constructed to tread the finest rail on the fence of political indecision." [3] Although the Balfour Declaration was ostensibly addressed to British Zionists through the medium of Lord Rothschild, actually it was a declaration to the Jews of the world and in particular to those in America, Russia and Germany because of their potential influence on the attitude of their respective governments in World War I. World wars seem to produce a spate of promissory notes on the Near East. The essential paragraph of the declaration read as follows:

> His Majesty's Government view with favour the establishment in Palestine of a National Home for the Jewish people, and will use their best endeavors to facilitate the achievement of this object, it being clearly understood that nothing shall be done which may prejudice the civil and religious

rights of existing non-Jewish communities in Palestine, or the rights and political status enjoyed by Jews in any other country.

It should be noted that before the Balfour Declaration was enunciated by the British Government it had been approved by President Wilson. It was written into the League of Nations' Mandate for Palestine, had been approved by the Vatican, and unanimously sanctioned by both Houses of the U.S. Congress.[4]

World War II found little difference in the equivocal attitude of the Great Powers. Faced with a life and death struggle, and this time with German forces actually in Arab lands in North Africa, and with the Mufti of Jerusalem, Haj Amin Husseini, practically a house-guest of Hitler, the beleaguered Allies sought of necessity to maintain friendly relations with the Arab governments. At the same time the world revulsion of feeling at the extermination of the Jews in Hitler's gas chambers predisposed public opinion in Britain, the United States, France and elsewhere in favor of the Zionist cause. It seemed reasonable to ask why indeed the Jews, who had been trying for a generation to establish a national home in Palestine, should not be permitted to do so. The result was a continuance of the World War I practice of saying one thing to one side and another thing to the other. President Roosevelt was the protagonist of this confusing policy.

For example, on May 26, 1943, a confidential note was sent to King Ibn Saud of Saudi Arabia asserting that no decision affecting the basic situation in Palestine would be reached "without full consultation with both Arabs and Jews."[5] In the next year, in February 1944, the Arab States protested against resolutions of the U.S. Congress calling for unlimited postwar Jewish immigration into Palestine;[6] but at the Chicago Convention in 1944 the Democratic Party declared, "We favor the opening of Palestine to unrestricted

Jewish immigration and colonization and such a policy as to
result in the establishment there of the free and democratic
Jewish Commonwealth." [7] Roosevelt supported this policy
and added the personal commitment that "if re-elected I
shall . . . help bring about its realization."

However, in the year 1945 President Roosevelt had met
privately on an American cruiser in the Suez Canal with King
Ibn Saud and had given assurances that "he would take no
action which . . . might prove hostile to the Arab people."
The author has since talked with the sole interpreter present
at this interview, which took place aboard the USS *Quincy*,
anchored in the Great Bitter Lake (appropriate spot!), February 12, 1945. This was the late Colonel William Eddy,
USMC, then American Naval Attaché at the Embassy in
Cairo, born in Sidon, who spoke native Arabic. Colonel
Eddy insisted in his recollection that no matter how carefully
Roosevelt chose his words, King Ibn Saud emerged from the
audience with the conviction that so long as Roosevelt was
President of the United States there would be no establish-
ment of a Jewish Commonwealth in Palestine.*

3.

With the end of the war in 1945 the question of what to do
about Palestine, already surcharged with political emotion,
became ever more burning bright. In May 1946 the Anglo-
American Commission of Inquiry established by the United
States and United Kingdom governments published its report, which was rejected out of hand by both the Zionists
and the members of the Arab League. Its principal recommendations were that 100,000 Jewish refugees from Europe

---

* This is borne out in a memorandum addressed to President Truman by
Acting Secretary of State Joseph C. Grew, in which he wrote, "In his meeting with King Ibn Saud, early in 1945, Mr. Roosevelt promised the King
that as regards Palestine he would make no move hostile to the Arab people and would not assist the Jews against the Arabs." [8]

should be admitted into Palestine over a period of over two years and that sale of land to Jews should no longer be restricted. It was prophetic that the British Chiefs of Staff thought that implementation of the report would lead to an Arab-Jewish War; and the U.S. Joint Chiefs of Staff thought that implementation of the report would invite repercussions beyond the control of British troops in the Middle East, but that it would be unwise to send U.S. troops to Palestine.[9] On the point of Arab hostility to any increase in Jewish influence in Palestine, Glubb Pasha, the commander of the Arab Legion of Transjordan, has testified to the hot resentment of the Arabs to ask why, if the U.S. and U.K. were so anxious to help the Jewish refugees, they did not take them into their own countries rather than send them to an Arab land.[10]

The Arab governments met twice to consider their line of action after the publication of the Anglo-American Commission's report. The first conferences of Arab heads of state met on June 2, 1946, at Inchass, one of King Farouk's country houses; but the more important conference of Arab leaders took place shortly afterward at Bludan in Syria. Here it was decided publicly to reject the Anglo-American Commission's recommendation on Palestine, while secretly the Arab delegates agreed that if the Zionists sought to achieve the Jewish State in Palestine by force this would be met by Arab force. In other words, the Bludan Conference was the beginning of an official Arab attitude which led within two years to war.[11]

We thus find the lines clearly drawn between both sides, Arab and Jew, with the big powers in some cases on the periphery and in others, as in the case of Britain and the United States, in the middle. In the forthcoming contest of will and of objectives the Jews had two immense advantages. First, they were united by millennia of oppression and by the recent searing experience of World War II. This persecution of the Jews by the Nazis had likewise solidified behind the Zionists a vast and influential bulk of non-Jewish world opinion. Secondly, the Jews were prepared to devote their resources worldwide to the support of the Jewish Agency in Palestine. In contrast, although the Arabs burned with a feeling of grievance and felt that the most monumental injustice in the world was on the point of perpetration in ousting Arabs from an Arab land to make way for alien intruders, the Arab governments were unable to work in unison. At no time in the war which ensued was there a joint doctrine or combined military operations or any effective coordination of Arab effort. This is cited because in the conduct of limited war the side which knows what it wants and how to achieve that objective has a great advantage over the other side which may know what it wants but not how to achieve it.*

We now enter into a period where, concentrated by the burning glass of destiny, all the elements of history entered into sharp focus on the map of Palestine. Events henceforth moved with the ineluctable cadence of a Greek tragedy.

This was the period of what Churchill once described as "the clattering down of the British Empire." We have already seen how British power at the end of World War II was so attenuated that in the case of the Greek Civil War the United Kingdom Government felt itself obliged almost to give an ultimatum to the United States in turning over its responsibilities for Greece to the stronger partner. So, too, it was with the liquidation of empire. Under the new Labour Government independence was granted to Burma and India. The increasing frustrations of Palestine urged a remorseless

---

* On this point Glubb Pasha makes a trenchant observation: "The Jews went from strength to strength, securing one partial concession after another, and every time growing more powerful. The Arabs always demanded all or nothing — and obtained nothing. If the Arabs had been as skillful as the Jews, the tragedy of the Arab refugees need never have occurred." [12]

logic that this unrewarding stewardship be relinquished. Finally, Britain decided to turn the whole muddle over to the United Nations.

Speaking in the House of Commons on February 18, 1947, Foreign Secretary Bevin said the Government had

> been faced with an irreconcilable conflict of principles. There are in Palestine about 1,200,000 Arabs and 600,000 Jews. For the Jews, the essential point of principle is the creation of a sovereign Jewish State. For the Arabs, the essential point of principle is to resist to the last the establishment of Jewish sovereignty in any part of Palestine. The discussions of the last month have quite clearly shown that there is no prospect of resolving this conflict by any settlement negotiated between the parties . . . We have, therefore, reached the conclusion that the only course now open to us is to submit the problem to the judgment of the United Nations . . . We shall then ask the United Nations . . . to recommend a settlement of the problem. We do not intend ourselves to recommend any particular solution . . .[13]

On April 2, 1947, Britain formally requested a special session of the U.N. General Assembly, which promptly convened. On May 15, 1947, the Assembly established a special Committee on Palestine, dubbed UNSCOP, made up of Australia, Canada, Czechoslovakia, Guatemala, India, Iran, the Netherlands, Peru, Sweden, Uruguay, and Yugoslavia. After months of taking testimony in Palestine, as had previous commissions of inquiry, the majority report of UNSCOP proposed the partition of Palestine into Jewish and Arab states to be bound by economic union. The map describing this Soloman's solution gave the new Jewish state the coast of Palestine from Haifa to below Tel Aviv, all of Western Galilee, and the triangular salient of the desert Negev. The Arabs were to have Eastern and Northern Galilee and the central plains and hills of Palestine plus the Gaza Strip. In addition, Jerusalem was to be internationalized with its pop-

ulation of 100,000 Jews and 105,000 Arabs. Although the
Zionists would have wished more from this solution, following the tactic acutely described by Glubb Pasha they opted
for the policy of half a loaf being better than no bread, while
the Arabs, true to character, violently rejected the entire
scheme. Ultimately, on November 29, 1947, the United Nations General Assembly voted for the partition of Palestine
as recommended by UNSCOP by a vote of 33 in favor, 13
against, the other U.N. delegations abstaining. Both the U.S.
and U.S.S.R. voted in the affirmative. The British Government announced that its administration would be withdrawn
from Palestine by May 15, 1948, and its troops by August 1.
Both sides now began to prepare for war, although on the
Jewish side few except Ben Gurion seemed to take seriously
the Arab threat of action, and the Arabs on their side were
divided yet dangerously over-confident.

4.

The Arab League held numerous meetings of chiefs of
government and at times heads of state. It met in Cairo on
March 23, 1947, in Sofar in Lebanon on September 16, and
at Aley, again in Lebanon, in October of 1947, at which time,
on paper at least, there was established an Arab General
Headquarters. Most of these meetings developed more disagreement than concord. Typical was the meeting of the
Arab Prime Ministers in Cairo on December 12, 1947, which
ended as usual in disagreement, with the Egyptians and
Saudis hanging back while King Abdullah of Transjordan
again indicated his intention of intervening with the Arab
Legion once the British Mandate ended.[14] Abdullah, in fact,
had already made his own preparations.

The King of Transjordan as early as November 1947 secretly met in his palace in Amman with Golda Myerson of
the Jewish Agency (later Mrs. Meir) to discuss prospects.
The King told the future Israeli Foreign Minister that he

would take over the Arab part of Palestine and then conclude a treaty with the new Jewish State.[15] Early in the next year Abdullah revealed the same intention to Foreign Minister Bevin. He sent his Prime Minister, Tewfik Pasha Abu Huda, with Glubb serving as translator. According to Glubb's account, Abdullah "proposed to send the Arab Legion across the Jordan when the British Mandate ended, and to occupy that part of Palestine awarded to the Arabs which was contiguous with the frontier of Trans-Jordan." Bevin replied, "It seems the obvious thing to do." He added, however, "But do not go and invade the areas allotted to the Jews." [16]

Abdullah was playing a farsighted and realistic game with the great advantages of knowing what he wanted, having a striking force upon which he could count, *Al Jeish al Arabi*, the Arab Legion, and the additional advantage of geographic propinquity to his objective. Above all, he coveted being King of Jerusalem. In this his arch-rival was the former Mufti, Haj Amin Husseini, the recent collaborator with Hitler. Another rival to Abdullah's ambition was Egypt, which had no desire to find the formerly insignificant Transjordan becoming a major Arab power.

While the Arabs debated and their hastily contrived General Headquarters drew up a war plan and conferred the title of Commander in Chief on an Iraqi General, Nur ad-Din Mahmoud, the Jews were busily and secretly preparing for war. They had an instrument at hand in the Haganah, the armed militia, whose striking force was the elite Palmach brigades. In addition, Ben Gurion took steps to secure arms and munitions. Emissaries were sent to France, Czechoslovakia, Canada and the United States to buy arms or at least, as in the case of the United States, to raise several million dollars in contributions from American Zionists to acquire the heavy machinery necessary for creating an armaments industry in the new Jewish State. After an agreement had been reached between Shertok and Gromyko in New York in January 1948 the Jewish Agency got the approval of the Czechoslovakian Government to sell arms. These were smuggled into Palestine disguised as tractors, foodstuffs, and other imports despite the fact that the Security Council in its resolution of April 17, 1948 had imposed a general arms embargo as well as a ban on the bringing in of potential fighting personnel to Palestine.[17]

Here a word might be said of the strenuous effort made by the U.S. Government to live up to the requirements of the Security Council's arms embargo. The zealous Zionists in the United States sought by every stratagem to accumulate arms for the forthcoming conflict. The author well remembers how one enterprising group even went so far as to attempt to purchase a surplus escort aircraft carrier from the U.S. Navy! As President Truman reports in his memoirs, "I do not think I ever had as much pressure and propaganda aimed at the White House as I had in this instance. The persistence of a few of the extreme Zionist leaders — actuated by political motives and engaging in political threats — disturbed and annoyed me." [18] In fact, the steadfastness with which the United States Government throughout sought to support the United Nations and sustain its actions in an effort, first to keep the peace, and second to restore the peace, goes far to refute the heated Arab claims that the United States was always subservient to "the Zionists."

5.

For months before the termination of the Mandate on May 15 extensive fighting had gone on between Arabs and Jews in Palestine with the British only rarely intervening to maintain an increasingly precarious state of security. By March 1958 the so-called Arab "Liberation Army" * numbered some 4000 men inside of Palestine. Its leader was a Lebanese free-

---

* One of the Arab Legion interpreters translated this as "the Salvation Army." [19]

booter named Fawsi el Kaukji who was later to reappear
murkily and briefly in the Lebanese Civil War of 1958. This
band later grew to some 7000 men, but their inept handling
by Kaukji and the determined counterattacks of the Haganah
and Palmach forces reduced the "Liberation Army" to a dis-
organized rabble. More stern fighting took place on the access routes to Jerusalem as both sides fought for control of
the means of communication.

Fierce fighting broke out in Haifa from April 20–22, 1948,
with the Haganah speedily gaining the upper hand. At a
conference between the leaders of the Arabs and Jews, the
Jewish Mayor of Haifa said the Jews did not want a single
inhabitant of the city to leave and stressed that the Arabs
could remain as equal citizens in every way. However, the
Arab leadership spurned this request and asked that the
Arab population should be permitted to leave the city. Thus
began the pattern which led to the still unresolved problem
of the Arab refugees, wards of the United Nations, unwanted
by Jew and Arab alike.

Elsewhere, as the fighting raged around isolated communities, the Arab population had already begun to flee Palestine.
Although technically this exodus was an Arab initiative, the
deliberate terrorist acts of the Irgun and Stern gangs undoubtedly contributed to the stampede of the Arabs who
were to spend the remainder of their lives as refugees. For
example, the massacre of the entire population of Deir Yas-
sen, where 250 dead bodies of men, women and children
were thrown down the village well, was calculated to strike
terror in the hearts of the Arab population of Palestine.[20]
Against such acts of outrage the prim map of partition
painted by UNSCOP became incarnadined with blood.

6.

On the eve of the end of the Mandate, as of May 14, in
rough fashion there had already taken place the division into

Jewish and Arab portions of Palestine as outlined by the General Assembly's resolution of November 29, 1947, with the exception of Western Galilee, where fighting still went on, and Jerusalem, which was still in Arab hands. According to one authority the line-up of opposing forces on the morning of May 15 was as follows:

The total strength of the invading armies was approximately 24,000, divided up in this way:

Egypt	10,000	
Arab Legion	4,500	
Syria	3,000	
Iraq	3,000	
Lebanon	3,000	(including 2000 men of the Arab Liberation Army)

Along the principal fronts the line-up reflected the same trend. This was the picture on the morning of May 15th:

	Israelis	Arabs	
South	5,000	5,000	Egyptians
Deep south and Hebron	1,500	4,000	Egyptians
Jerusalem and corridor	4,500	4,000	Arab Legion
		1,000	Egyptians
Central front: Tel Aviv			
Natanya	3,000	3,000	Iraqis
North	5,000	3,000	Syrians
		1,000	Lebanese
		2,000	A.L.A.
Total	19,000	23,000	[21]

Glubb gives identical figures for the Arab forces.[22]

The Arabs who had their last "summit meeting" at Amman, April 30, 1948, were on the surface united in their resolve to destroy the Jews but secretly remained divided. Years later the then President of Lebanon, General Fuad Chehab, who had been Commander in Chief of the Lebanese armed forces at the time of the Israeli War, confided to the author the vast disarray of intent and capability among the Arab military leaders, which was merely a reflection of a similar division among the Arab politicians.

The Arab leadership can probably be divided into three categories: those who definitely intended to intervene, such as King Abdullah and the ex-Mufti of Jerusalem and possibly the Syrians; those who might be called "pseudo-interventionists," in which category would certainly come the Lebanese and the Iraqis; and finally those who did not want to intervene at all despite their fervored speeches. In this category were definitely Saudi Arabia and, possibly at the beginning, Egypt. Later, however, as events proved, Egypt decided to intervene, probably to forestall Abdullah's ambition.

On the Jewish side there was the great advantage of unity of purpose and one objective, the independence of the new State of Israel. On May 14, the day before the Mandate officially expired, the Jewish National Council proclaimed the establishment of the State of Israel. On the same day President Truman gave *de facto* recognition to the Provisional Government of Israel.[23]

7.

The official war in Palestine was not long in coming. The Egyptian Government on May 15 formally advised the Secretary General of the United Nations that its troops were crossing the Palestine border "to restore order." Early on the morning of that day three Egyptian Spitfires came out of the sun over Tel Aviv and bombed the power station. Attack on Arab initiative was exactly what the Israelis wanted.

The remainder of the war can be described briefly. It

consisted of an initial struggle between the Israelis, the Egyptians and the Transjordanian Arab Legion which ended with the Security Council Truce of June 11 when both sides were breathless and badly needed respite; a brief, fierce nine-day period of renewed fighting early in July, when the Israelis took a thousand square kilometres of Arab-held territory, including a corridor from Tel Aviv to Jerusalem and the important Arab towns of Lydda and Ramle; to be followed by another cease-fire effective July 18. This uneasy truce was broken in October by a determined Israeli drive into the Negev, the obliging Egyptians once more affording a pretext by attacking a convoy which moved under a U.N. safe-conduct. The fighting in the Negev was interrupted by another Security Council cease-fire resolution effective October 22; and the final action terminated with the Israeli "Operation Horev," launched on December 23, which cut off the Egyptians in the Gaza Strip. In other words, the fighting in Palestine was a seesaw motion, punctuated by brief periods of respite when both sides found it convenient to obey the dictates of the Security Council to stop fighting. During these breathing spells both sides industriously sought to improve their position in matériel and weapons.* In ad-

---

* This is most graphically shown by the following table on the changes which had taken place in the armament of the Israeli Army between May 15 and October 12.

	May 15th 1948	October 12th 1948
Men	85,000	80,000
Guns	4	250
120 mm. mortars	none	12
6-inch mortars	none	88
3-inch mortars	105	889
2-inch mortars	682	618
Davidka mortars	16	22
PIATS and anti-tank rifles	75	675
Machine guns	1,550	7,550
Rifles	22,000	60,000
Sub-machine guns	11,000	21,300[24]

dition the Israelis had created a piebald air force, ranging
from a few renegade Flying Fortresses to Spitfires and Mes-
serschmitts. They had no lack of ex-World War II pilots. On
the Arab side their initial superiority in the British 25-
pounder gun was at last counterbalanced by the Israeli in-
genuity in imports.

Meanwhile the Security Council had appointed a Mediator
in the hope that a single dispassionate neutral man could intervene between these fiercely warring Semite factions. The
Mediator chosen was Count Folke Bernadotte, a scion of the
royal house of Sweden who had distinguished himself, not
only as head of the Swedish Red Cross, but in playing a significant role in the negotiations with Himmler at the end of
World War II. He and his Deputy, Dr. Ralph Bunche, arrived at their headquarters on the Island of Rhodes just before the truce of June 11 became effective. The Mediator
worked tirelessly and with painstaking devotion to attempt
to devise a solution which would be acceptable to both sides.
He failed and his "Bernadotte Plan" was rejected by both
Jew and Arab. Count Bernadotte likewise paid for his devotion with his life. On September 17, in the streets of Jerusalem while traveling under an official Israeli *laissez passer* he
was assassinated by members of the Stern Gang. *

The end of the Arab-Israeli War came clearly in sight with
the successful Israeli thrust into the Negev which began in
mid-October. Although the Egyptians put up a valiant resistance and defended themselves well in fixed points, their

---

* The writer, who had been on consultation with Count Bernadotte three
days before in Rhodes, made the following note: "Count Bernadotte was
murdered in Jerusalem on the afternoon of Friday the 17th by five members
of the Stern Gang who placed a jeep across the path of his three cars, which
were traveling in the Jewish-held Katamon District of the City and were
under an official Israeli safe conduct. They jumped out, ran to his car,
which was last in line, and shot him through the heart with a Sten gun. He
and a senior French U.N. military observer, Colonel Serot, who was sitting
beside him, were killed instantly." The author subsequently sent Countess
Bernadotte, born the American Estelle Manville, the last photograph taken
of her husband on the Island of Rhodes.

line of communications was cut. One of the young officers who fought most bravely with the Egyptian Brigade Group surrounded at Faluja was Major Gamal Abdul Nasser. His *Achates fideles,* Major Hakim Amer, had fought with equal courage under Colonel Naguib in the earlier thrust toward Tel Aviv.

The fighting in the Negev ended pursuant to another Security Council cease-fire effective October 22. On the 11th of November the Council called for a permanent armistice to replace its frequently riddled truces, but Egypt refused even a truce. On this pretext the Israelis launched their final drive, "Operation Horev," on December 23, which resulted in cutting the line of communications of the Egyptian forces in the Gaza Strip, thus isolating the Gaza army from the rest of Egypt. This was on January 3, 1949. On the 6th the Egyptian Government announced its readiness to enter into armistice negotiations at the headquarters of Dr. Bunche, the Acting U.S. Mediator at Rhodes. On January 7 all firing ceased on the southern front and the war between Israel and Egypt had come to an end.[25]

The Egyptian-Israeli general armistice agreement was signed at Rhodes on February 24, 1949. On March 23, an armistice was concluded with Lebanon and on July 20 with Syria. When on March 20 Israeli troops had reached the Gulf of Aqaba, Transjordan signed a cease-fire agreement on Rhodes. The armistice negotiations with Jordan were then secretly transferred to King Abdullah's winter palace at Shuna near the Dead Sea. After almost a week of negotiations, at last a map was drawn up by Brigadier Coker, Glubb's operations officer, and approved by King Abdullah. On April 3 an armistice incorporating this agreement was formally signed in the presence of Dr. Bunche.[26]

Although it was believed at the time that these armistice agreements were merely temporary arrangements to be speedily supervened by permanent peace treaties, this did not transpire. Instead, the armistice agreements have become a sort of *de facto* peace between Israel and the Arab States, supervised by the United Nations. Nevertheless, because they are armistice agreements and not peace treaties a pretext has been given to the Arab governments for maintaining that they are "still at war with Israel." In the event, however, since the armistice agreements have so long endured and a sort of peace has been more or less preserved (with the punctuation of border skirmishes and the one week's war in Sinai in 1956), the historian may be content with the French phrase, "*Il n'y a que le provisoire qui dure.*"

8.

In conclusion of this account of one of the most dramatic and emotionally surcharged limited wars which have taken place in the twentieth century, it first of all can be stated that both sides knew what they wanted. The Jews wanted to establish a state in Palestine for their national home and the Arabs, fearful of the Jews' drive, intelligence, and worldwide resources, were determined to oppose this "to the death." Also the Arabs felt an irremediable sense of injustice that in a country where the ratio of Arabs to Jewish inhabitants was two to one, the Arabs should be cast out to make room for aliens from over the sea.

Although both sides knew what they wanted, one side knew better how to achieve its objectives. The Jews mobilized their resources totally, not only their human and material assets in Palestine, but throughout the world and especially in the United States, where not only was popular sentiment largely in favor of the establishment of Israel but also private Jewish monetary resources of great magnitude were available.

The Arabs, despite the universality of their hatred, mobilized only partially. In Palestine, their human resources were critically demoralized and a vast exodus of refugees took place. In the Arab world, although armies were got together, there was no central coordination of the war and rivalries between one government and another were all too evident. Furthermore, in contrast to the Jews, who had mobilized world opinion largely on their side, there was no equally effective marshaling of Moslem opinion and aid on the Arab side.[27]

Although the Jewish total objective was the establishment of a Jewish State, Israel, the Jews were content to fix their eyes on limited objectives and inch by inch to get as much as they could by military and diplomatic means, retaining the fruits of their victory with the blessing of the United Nations.

While this was a limited war by the confines of the area and the forces involved, in another sense it was an almost unlimited war by virtue of external Jewish support for Israel and the European and American interest in establishing European Jewish refugees conveniently in a "national home" far from American and European shores. No other state so depends as does Israel on external support and private financing.

One consequence has been the unanimous Arab opinion that United States policy is controlled by Jews. That this is not the case does not prevail against Arab emotions; and in the Arab East the silhouette profile of "Uncle Sam" protrudes a Semitic nose.*

---

* A brief illustration will suffice. In 1960 the Moslem Prime Minister of Lebanon, Saeb Salem, went to New York City to head his delegation to the United Nations. He was invited by the Overseas Writers Club to address that body at a luncheon, but when the next day he looked in the New York papers for the report of his speech it was nowhere to be found. To this day the Prime Minister is convinced that Jewish influence on the American press forced deletion of any reference to his address. That this was not the fact is well known to New York editors, but nothing will shake Saeb Salem's convictions on this point. Therefore the Arab article of faith that American policy is controlled by Jews is a political fact, whether or not it is an historical one.

Despite this conviction of the Arabs, the war in Sinai in 1956 forced a rude awakening on the government of Israel. Ben Gurion and his counselors had planned that the amphibious landings at Port Said should take place on the very day of the American presidential elections on the fond hypothesis that President Eisenhower, who was a candidate for reelection, would be too preoccupied to react adversely to what was happening at Suez. This massive miscalculation and the world reaction to the fiasco at Suez may have shown the Israeli leaders that they cannot draw indefinitely on an imagined credit of good will in the Free World.

Nevertheless, the lessons of the American landings in Lebanon in 1958 indicated that the United States would support small independent nations of the Near East who sought to defend their integrity from attack. This lesson has not been lost either upon Arab leaders or those of Israel. Both the Suez and Lebanese aspects of limited war will be the subject of the next two chapters.

Current problems include the intent of Israel to take what it regards to be its fair share of the waters of the River Jordan and the equal Arab determination to frustrate this ambition. It is a tragedy that the equitable technical recommendations of the Eric Johnston report on a fair sharing of the Jordan waters, although once accepted by the Arab engineers, were rejected by the Arab politicians.

The problem of the Arab refugees remains a festering wound on the conscience of the world. Although the Israelis are technically correct in saying that the refugees put themselves into their present condition by stampeding and fleeing under fire from Palestine, the fact remains that many stampeded because of Jewish acts of terrorism, and Israel has done practically nothing to contribute to the amelioration of the lot of these wretched former residents. The Arab governments, for their part, have done little other than to offer acreage in their countries upon which the refugees have been sustained in camps by the United Nations UNRWA with a majority of U.S. financial support. Ultimately, the solution will probably be in technical training of the second generation of the refugees and readiness by the Arab governments to accept these skilled people into their respective economies. In fact, the trend is now discernible: today only about 40 per cent of the refugees drawing full or partial UNRWA support live inside camps.

Danger remains in the escalation of armed forces on both sides and the increasingly lethal character of these forces. In the case of Israel, French Mystère jets replace older aircraft and are balanced on the Egyptian side by newer editions of the Russian MIG. Eventually, the world will have to take a close look at the possibility of nuclear proliferation. The Israelis undoubtedly have the scientific capacity and modern reactor at Dimona. However, the Egyptians have had expert German scientific advice in rocketry.

In the long run the one unifying emotion among the Arabs has been their hatred and fear of Israel. This may over the years result in some more constructive form of unity. Israel continues to exist as an independent colony of West and East, an enclave behind barbed wire on the coast of the Arab world. Yet over the years time heals all wounds and a new generation of Semites, Arabs and Jews may come to see the advantages of working together. They may even recall Voltaire's observation that "One should not always be harping upon the small differences which separate us but on the great qualities which unite us."

Although one of the characteristics of limited war in the last half of the twentieth century is the widespread use of surrogate forces, in the war for Israeli independence there was a direct confrontation of Arab versus Jew. In a wider sense, however, from the aspect of the world balance of power as between the U.S.S.R. and the United States, it might be argued that the Soviet Union abetted the play of surrogate forces on the theory that any conflict breeding trouble in the Near East over a period of decades might be useful from the Communist point of view. Certainly, it was for this reason that the U.S.S.R. voted affirmatively on the U.N. resolution of November 29, 1947, and, by the Gromyko-Shertok Agreement early in 1948, made it possible for Czechoslovakia to furnish arms and munitions to the Jewish Agency, thus in large measure underwriting the success of the war against the Arabs. Subsequent Soviet military assistance to the U.A.R. likewise via Czechoslovakia, insured that the Arab side would in future have a military counterweight to Israel and thus underwrite the prospect of continuing turmoil in the neuralgic tri-continental crossroads of the Middle East.

That trouble was yet in store on the tri-continental bridge was revealed in 1956, in Sinai and Suez.

CHAPTER VI

Sinai and Suez, 1956

1.

WHEN SIR ANTHONY EDEN was resting on the island of Jamaica after the episode at Suez, he occupied a house loaned to him by Ian Fleming. Surely there must have been a temptation in reflecting on recent events to wonder how James Bond might have dealt with this episode.

Many of the chapters of this study on limited war are devoted to an examination of limited wars contrived by the Communists against the Free World. In the case of Suez, however, we have an instance of limited war planned by two leading powers in the NATO alliance and carefully plotted by those two powers with a third state, Israel. We also have in the Israeli campaign of "Operation Kadesh" a case study of limited war for clearly defined objectives, with a plan of delicate modulation permitting the Israeli Government to attain limited objectives or more general ones, depending on the political climate in which the military operation was carried out.

It all began with the financing of the high Aswan Dam. Egypt, a land of 23 million people, had exactly 6 million *feddans* (acres) of cultivated land to feed its people. With the increase in population each year, it was clearly necessary to put more of the Nile Valley under irrigation, and this could only be accomplished by the high dam long projected at Aswan. It was estimated that the project would cost $1.5 billion. Studies were undertaken by the World Bank at the request of the Egyptian Government, and the United States and the United Kingdom were asked to make a joint loan to Egypt of which $56 million would be provided by the United States and $14 million by Britain. The World Bank was expected to offer a loan of $200 million for the initial stage of the project.

These offers of aid were made in December, 1955, undoubtedly to counter an anticipated upsurge of Soviet influence after the announcement in September 1955 by President Nasser that Egypt had signed an agreement with the Soviet Union for the supply of Czech arms (after previous requests of the United States and Great Britain had been refused). Soviet technicians were to be sent to train the Egyptian armed forces in the use and maintenance of these weapons and Egyptian officers were to take special courses at a Warsaw Pact training ground in Poland. Almost simultaneously, the Syrian Government announced that it too had placed an order for Soviet Bloc arms which for convenience were to be sent along with the Egyptian matériel. It soon became apparent that the contract for payment of these weapons would come to $450 million for Egypt and $100 million for Syria.

The Soviet Union offered Egypt not only aid in war matériel but likewise in the financing of the new Aswan Dam. The Soviet Foreign Minister, Shepilov, arrived in Egypt on June 18, 1956, a week after the evacuation by British forces of the Suez base, and offered Nasser a loan of $1.5 billion, the full price of the Aswan Dam project, to be repaid over sixty years at 2 per cent.[2] However, despite this offer, the Egyptian Ambassador to the United States, Ahmed Hussein, returned to Washington on July 17 and announced that his government had decided to go ahead with the U.S.–U.K. loans supplemented by the credit from the World Bank.

Meanwhile, however, the attitude of Washington had hardened. The arms deal with the Soviet Union seemed to make it economically impossible for Egypt, whose sole export crop was cotton, to accumulate the necessary reserves of foreign exchange, both to pay for Communist arms and for service on the Free World loans for the Aswan Dam. In consequence, on July 19, Secretary of State Dulles informed the Egyptian Ambassador that the deal was off.[3] The text of the Secretary of State's note to the Egyptian Ambassador was at once released to the press and at the same time the Foreign Office in London announced that the United Kingdom had decided that it would not participate in the Aswan project. *

2.

Nasser heard this news on the island of Brioni where he and Nehru had been the guests of Tito. Nasser, accompanied by Nehru, immediately returned to Cairo, where Nehru issued a statement condemning Britain and the United States. On July 24, at a ceremony for the opening of a new pipeline near Cairo, Nasser made an incendiary speech, in which he shouted, "I look at Americans and I say — 'Americans may you choke on your fury.'" After the speech, the Soviet Ambassador, Kisselev, said, "We are now ready to finance the dam if Egypt wishes it." [4]

* Secretary of State Dulles was later to explain in his press conference of April 2, 1957 (State Department Bulletin Vol. 36, April 22, 1957), "Then there was the further fact that the Egyptians had during the immediately preceding period been developing ever-closer relations with the Soviet bloc countries . . .

"And in that way the Egyptians, in a sense, forced upon us an issue to which I think there was only one proper response. That issue was, do nations which play both sides get better treatment than nations which are stalwart and work with us?"

He was not long in receiving an answer.

Two days later in a speech in Alexandria on Thursday, July 26, commemorating the third anniversary of the Egyptian revolution, Nasser announced that the Suez Canal would be nationalized and its revenues used for financing the Aswan Dam. As he spoke, when he pronounced the key word, "De-Lesseps," the Egyptian Government occupied the Canal Zone and took over the installations of the Canal Company.[5]

The reaction in London and Paris was swift. In an emergency meeting of the British Cabinet on the early morning of Friday, July 27, at which the diplomatic representatives of the United States and France were present, Eden said, "The Egyptian has his thumb on our windpipe. Tell Mr. Dulles I cannot allow that."[6] Robert Murphy, the Deputy Under Secretary of State for Political Affairs, was immediately dispatched to London by President Eisenhower with instructions to "hold the fort." The Foreign Secretary, Selwyn Lloyd, made it clear that the British Government had decided to use force if necessary. On the evening of his arrival, Murphy dined with his old colleague, Harold Macmillan, the Chancellor of the Exchequer. Present at the dinner was Field Marshal Lord Alexander. Neither of the distinguished Britons made any secret of their belief that a military operation could be mounted in August, that it would take only a few divisions and would last only ten days. "Nasser has to be chased out of Egypt," said they.[7]

Other governments shared this view. Obviously, the one most intimately concerned was the Government of Israel, which had studied with growing alarm the dimensions of the Egyptian-Syrian arms deal with the Soviet Bloc. As early as late September 1955, Shimon Peres, Director General of the Israeli Ministry of Defense, had had secret conversations in Paris with the then Minister of Interior, Maurice Bourgès-Maunoury, who was also responsible for Algerian Affairs. It was not difficult for the Israeli functionary and the French Minister to agree that Nasser was providing assistance to the Algerian rebels and that both governments had a common cause against him.[8]

France likewise had an economic concern in Suez. The Compagnie Universelle Du Canal De Suez was *une vieille dame très riche*. As one French writer has put it, its shareholders were *"bien heureux mortels"* — because in any given year one-third of the company's income was distributed to the stockholders.[9]

In consequence, it was with understandable emotion that at 11 o'clock on the morning of July 27, Prime Minister Guy Mollet telephoned Sir Anthony Eden to confirm the desire of France to take part in any attack against Egypt which the British Government might prepare. The French Prime Minister also proposed Israeli collaboration, which Eden rejected because of obvious complications in Britain's relations with other Arab states.[10]

In judging the decisions taken by governments it is important to discern between myth and reality. However, certain fixations of thought, whether erroneous or not, must be rated as political facts, and it is against this background that judgments of statesmen must be evaluated. There was no doubt at all of the strategic importance to Britain and France, as well as other countries, of the Suez Canal. There was also no gainsaying the fact that 60 per cent of the crude oil used by Britain and France came through the Canal from the Persian Gulf. The economy of Western Europe largely depended upon the hydrocarbon fuels from this part of the world, sent either through the Suez Canal or by the two pipelines which debouch in the Levant: the IPC from Iraq, a two-headed line terminating both in Syria and in Lebanon, and the American TAPLINE from Daharan, ending at ancient Sidon in Lebanon.

But in addition there were concepts of Nasser which were

deeply etched in acid in the minds of the Prime Ministers of Great Britain and France. To Eden, Nasser was a potential Hitler; or failing that, he was a Mussolini subject to the Hitler-type influence of the U.S.S.R.[11] To Guy Mollet, Nasser was an arch-conspirator helping vigorously France's enemies in Algeria. To both Prime Ministers, the seizure of the Suez Canal seemed to present "another Munich." If they should be irresolute before this threat, the situation was irremediable.

The United States took a calmer view of the situation. At any event, it was not so dependent on the Suez Canal, either strategically or from the aspect of oil. Furthermore, the United States was ready to contemplate Egypt's right of nationalization, provided that there were safeguards for the international use of the Canal on reasonable terms for all nations. Primary in U.S. policy was the conviction of President Eisenhower that fundamental principles were involved and that the United States would not be a party to the use of force in view of its support of the rule of law and of the United Nations Charter. In consequence, when Secretary of State Dulles, who had been absent in Lima to attend the inauguration of the new Peruvian President, reached London on August 1, he bore very specific instructions from the President to prevent military intervention at Suez.[12]

On the diplomatic front, in the third week of August representatives of the eight signatory powers of the Constantinople Convention of 1888, plus fourteen other nations, met in London to approve an Anglo-American-French proposal for an international authority to operate the Canal. The London Conference appointed Prime Minister Menzies of Australia to head a delegation to propose this solution to Nasser, who promptly rejected it, on the ground that an international authority charged with operating a canal wholly within Egyptian territory would be prejudicial to Egypt's full sovereignty. However, Nasser made a counter suggestion that the users of the Canal should have their rights reaffirmed in a new treaty to replace the old 1888 Convention guaranteeing unrestricted passage through the Canal for all nations. All he insisted upon was that they pay tolls to Egypt. Meanwhile, the Canal continued to function smoothly despite nationalization, and some of the principal users of the Canal — e.g., the Norwegians — seemed so unconcerned that a conference of Norwegian shipmasters, held at the Norwegian Embassy at London, came to the unanimous conclusion that they could take their own ships through the Canal if necessary without the use of pilots, Egyptian or otherwise.[13]

3.

Meanwhile the British, French and Israeli governments prepared for war. Despite the vigor of their conversations on the morning after the sequestration of the Suez Canal, neither the British nor French government was prepared for immediate military action. In fact, the only ready-at-hand instrument for the instant application of force in the Mediterranean was the United States Sixth Fleet. The French were occupied and preoccupied in Algiers and the British simply did not have the wherewithal in amphibious lift, airborne capability, and armor instantly to place a punitive expedition en route to Suez. However, the French and British General Staffs were immediately instructed by their governments to prepare a plan for joint operations against Egypt. The proposed task force would be integrated under a British Supreme Commander with a French Deputy. Sir Charles Keightley, British Commander, Middle East, was named the Chief of "Operation Musketeer" and his Deputy was Admiral Barjot. The British land forces commander was General Stockwell, seconded by the French General Beaufre.* On the British side, there were 45,000 men, 12,000 vehicles, 300 aircraft and 100 warships of the Royal Navy, including five aircraft carriers, eventually got together for "Operation Musketeer." The French disposed of 34,000 men, 9,000 vehicles, 200 aircraft and 30 warships, including two aircraft carriers and the last battleship in active commission, the *Jean Bart*.[14]

These forces, impressive though the muster sounds, could be used only with difficulty. The closest base was Cyprus, but Cyprus is an island with few and inadequate ports.† In consequence, the main body of troops to be landed on the beaches of Egypt had to be stationed in Malta, and Malta is six days' convoy steaming by sea. The airborne troops, however, could easily be based on Cyprus. The greatest drawback in plan "Musketeer" was the length of time it took to assemble the various military components of two of the supposedly greatest powers of the Free World. Had the British and French been able to strike instantly after Nasser's speech on July 26, the verdict might have been different. Furthermore, in drawing up their objectives they seem to have overlooked the ancient axiom that when you strike at a king you must kill him.

The Anglo-French war objectives were simple. On the strategic side it was to control and keep control of the Suez Canal. The political objective was the wiping out of Nasser,

---

* Général d'Armée André Beaufre, with whom the author has discussed this chapter, makes the point that despite these command echelons he succeeded in maintaining an independent command of the French land forces. He had a liaison military mission in Tel Aviv. He also urged on General Keightley his own "Plan A" as contrasted with "Plan B" of Operation Musketeer, which was actually followed. This called for the amphibious forces to sortie from Cyprus rather than Malta. He never received a direct answer from either London or Paris, where the Ministers' reply was, "*Débrouillez-vous*."

† As the author well knows, after three passages under sail between Beirut and Famagusta.

with the corollary from the French point of view of eliminating Egypt as a base of supply for the Algerian rebels.

The Israeli war aims were perhaps equally simple but better modulated. "Operation Kadesh" was designed to be played like an accordion — it could be stretched out to the maximum or pressed tightly in. The objectives of the Israeli high command could be modest as, for example, merely the capture of the Gaza Strip and the opening of the Gulf of Aqaba by taking the Egyptian fortifications at Sharm-El-Sheikh. However, if wider victory awaited and Israel could destroy the Egyptian Army in Sinai, there was no telling what ultimate gains might be consolidated. This would depend upon the fate of arms and upon the attitude of world society.

The problem from the British point of view was how to get Israel into a conflict with Egypt without at the same time making Great Britain seem an ally of the Israelis against the Arabs. A constant concern at 10 Downing Street was a possibility that Israel would engage in hostilities with Jordan, an ally of the United Kingdom. In fact, a principal nightmare of Sir Anthony Eden must have been the prospect of Britain having to come to the assistance of its Jordanian ally against an Israel supported by France. According to one French authority, an agreement was signed on October 10, 1956, between the general staffs of France and Israel, allying France to Israel. Prior to this date, however, arrangements had been made for the training of Israeli Air Force pilots in France and for the supply of Mystère jets to Israel. French instructors were sent to train the Israelis on maintenance of equipment and spare parts, drawn from NATO stocks by France and shipped secretly to Israel.* [15]

---

*President Eisenhower reports in the second volume of his memoirs, *Waging Peace*, page 56, that "High-flying reconnaissance planes revealed that the Israeli had *sixty* French Mystère airplanes, not twelve, as the French had reported to us." *Op. cit.* footnote 12.

4.

We now emerge upon one of the most bizarre and yet fundamental developments of the Suez affair. This is what one commentator has ironically termed "the Treaty of Sèvres." [16]

The "Suez Affair" here assumes the silhouette of an iceberg — one-ninth above the surface and eight-ninths below. While so far as world attention was concerned, the British and French seemed intent on lodging their complaint against Egypt in the Security Council of the United Nations, at the same time, secret military talks were going on between the British and French in a joint study of the contemplated Israeli plan of attack. In fact, General Challe of the French General Staff arrived in London on October 12 with the Israeli plan and it was studied there until the 19th of October.

At the same time, Eden says in his memoirs that as for taking the Suez issue to the United Nations, "we were pledged and we intended to keep our word. The questions before us were when and in what form we should do so." [17] The "when" was October 14, and the "form" was a resolution in two parts. The first consisted of a statement of six basic principles governing the free and open transit for all nations through the Suez Canal, the manner of fixing of tolls and charges to be decided by agreement between Egypt and the users. The second part of the resolution called for the so-called Canal Users Association to receive the dues payable by the ships of its members and to cooperate with the Egyptian nationalized Canal Authority for the satisfactory management of the Suez Canal. This operative part of the resolution was vetoed by the U.S.S.R.

On October 16, according to Eden's memoirs, he and the Foreign Secretary flew to Paris to see Mollet and Pineau. Says Eden, "During recent months, we had been mounting our military preparations to deal with any interference or any other act by Nasser against our ships or our people. Now Nasser's policies were provoking Israel beyond endurance and this also we had to prepare for." [18]

This, indeed, the British and the French governments prepared for. The question from Eden's point of view was to find a *ruse de guerre*, which would justify military intervention under the pretext of preventing a conflict between Israel and Egypt. The plan was finally perfected between October 22 and 24. On the first of these dates, an Israeli airplane landed secretly on the military field of Villacoublay outside of Paris. Its passengers included the Israeli Prime Minister, Ben Gurion, the Commander in Chief, Moshe Dayan, and the ubiquitous Shimon Peres. The French Minister of Defense, Bourgés-Maunoury, lodged the party secretly in a villa at Sèvres.

Exceedingly detailed plans had already been worked out between the French land forces commander, General André Beaufre, and the Israeli Attaché in Paris, Colonel Nishri, for French air support of the contemplated Israeli thrust toward the Canal in the Sinai Peninsula. For instance, French aircraft based on Cyprus were to parachute provisions, anti-tank artillery and water to the Israeli forces and French naval fire support was to be assured on the coast of the Gaza Strip. The main preoccupation of Ben Gurion was the threat of aerial bombardment on Israeli towns once the attack had been launched. In consequence, it was of the utmost importance to him that assurances be given of British readiness to destroy the Egyptian air arm at the earliest possible moment.

Ben Gurion was likewise deeply concerned with "the danger of peace." During the very days that the Israelis were conferring at Sèvres with the British and French, in New York the activities of U.N. Secretary General Hammarskjöld had brought the Egyptian Foreign Minister and British and French diplomats into negotiations which seemed almost on the point of agreement.

The detailed plan agreed to at Sèvres forecast an exceedingly tight timetable. The Israeli attack was to begin on October 29 and end with the Anglo-French seaborne assault at dawn on November 6. This was the date of the United States Presidential election.* It was also the earliest date when, after six days' steaming from Malta, the amphibious forces could land at Port Said.

The agreed plan was in effect "Operation Kadesh" as it later developed in the event, with the exception that the Israelis ran ahead of their own timetable. In essence, the Israeli forces would attack the Sinai Peninsula in strength, the British Air Force would bomb the Egyptian planes on their airfields and the Anglo-French landings would be announced as for the protection of the Canal against both Israel and Egypt. An ultimatum of twelve hours' duration would call upon both sides to cease hostilities, which Israel would accept, hopefully, after it had reached a line ten miles east of the Canal. The ultimatum would not, however, be delivered until an Israeli radio news bulletin indicated that the advance units were at the approaches of the Canal. They would then have twelve hours to meet the ten-mile line. Once the main body of British and French troops had landed by sea on November 6 it was expected that the Canal Zone

* But the Israeli Prime Minister had been emphatically warned by President Eisenhower ten days before that "Ben-Gurion should not make any grave mistakes based upon his belief that winning a domestic election is as important to us as preserving and protecting the interests of the United Nations and other nations of the free world in that region. The Secretary [of State] is to point out, moreover [to Israeli Ambassador Abba Eban], that even if Ben-Gurion, in an aggressive move, should get an immediate advantage in the region, that on a long-term basis aggression on his part can not fail to bring catastrophe and such friends as he would have left in the world, no matter how powerful, could not do anything about it." Eisenhower, *Waging Peace*, p. 677.

from Port Said to Suez would be completely occupied by November 12.

According to Pineau, the agreement was incorporated in a formal document, signed by Patrick Dean for the United Kingdom, Ben Gurion for Israel, and himself for France. Said Pineau, quite understandably, "We decided that the agreement should never be published." [19]

After such minute and careful preparation at Sèvres it was easy for Eden to recall in his memoirs that "on October 25, the Cabinet discussed the specific possibility of conflict between Israel and Egypt and decided in principle how it would react if this occurred." [20] Small wonder that Robert Murphy, in his memoirs, in commenting on the official reason for the British-French expedition as being to safeguard the Canal and stop the Israeli-Egyptian fighting, wryly remarked, "Under the circumstances, this explanation was less than convincing." [21]

And President Eisenhower, in the recently published second volume of his memoirs, quotes Prime Minister Mollet in an after-aside: "If your government was not informed of the final developments, the reason . . . was our fear that if we had consulted it, it would have prevented us from acting." [22]

An appreciation of the situation made to President Eisenhower by Secretary of State Dulles November 1 was generally accurate although not prescient: " 'Israel mobilized and struck. We believed that Israel would attack Jordan, not Egypt,' he said. 'The Anglo-Jordanian Treaty probably prevented that attack and caused Britain, France, and Israel to agree on an Israeli strike against Egypt and on the British and French use of this strike as a pretext to protect the Canal. In all probability,' the Secretary went on, 'these moves were concerted; the French did the planning, the British acquiesced, and the French, in violation of the 1950 agree-

ment [on limitation of arms in the Near East], covertly supplied the Israelis with arms.' " * 23

<h1 style="text-align:center">5.</h1>

The attack on Suez, so carefully planned and rehearsed,
went off on schedule. The Israelis crossed into the Sinai on
the night of October 28 and "Operation Kadesh," supported
by the French air and naval arms, proceeded ahead of the
timetable. Four Israeli columns pushed into the Sinai:
Laskov's Brigade along the coast through the Gaza Strip, the
Seventh Armored Brigade along the old Turkish Road past
El-Auja, Sharon's 202nd Brigade along the Pilgrim Route to
the Mitla Pass which had been taken by parachutists, and
Yaffe's Brigade pushing south along the Gulf of Aqaba to
join later with Sharon's forces at Sharm-El-Sheikh at the
entrance to the Gulf of Aqaba.

The Anglo-French ultimata were duly issued to the Israeli
and Egyptian governments, calling upon them to withdraw
their forces and cease fighting within twelve hours: the
ultimatum to each expired at dawn on October 31. Particularly intriguing to world opinion was the demand upon
Egypt that it withdraw from its own territory. Understandably Nasser refused. He told the British Ambassador, Sir
Humphrey Trevelyan, "We are going to fight. The last time
we let you British in on a temporary basis, you stayed for
more than seventy years. I won't have that happen again." 25

Although massive British bombardment of the Egyptian

---

* Later President Eisenhower noted for Friday, November 2: "We received
a report from Assistant Secretary William Rountree in the State Department
recounting a conversation between Ambassador Douglas Dillon and French
Foreign Minister Pineau in which Pineau outlined step by step the whole
history of French collusion in the Suez crisis.

" 'Were the British involved?' Secretary Dulles asked.

" 'Oh yes,' Rountree assured him." 24

air bases did not begin until the expiration of the ultimatum on October 31, Eden himself reports that prior to British engagement in hostilities, four Canberras had been up over Cairo and the Canal following the Israeli thrust into Sinai. It was probably the threat of the Canberras based on Cyprus which caused Nasser to withdraw his Ilyushin bombers to bases in upper Egypt.

When the British attacked the air base complex around Cairo they also dropped leaflets calling on the Egyptians to oppose Nasser and threatening them with bombardment because they had permitted Nasser to come to power.

Meanwhile, with first news of Israeli attack into the Sinai, the Security Council met on October 30 and adopted a U.S. resolution supported by the U.S.S.R. calling on Israel to withdraw its forces from Egyptian territory, and upon all members of the U.N. to refrain from force or the threat of it. This resolution was vetoed by the United Kingdom and France. Following a second British-French veto in the Security Council, a resolution introduced by Yugoslavia was adopted convoking a special session of the General Assembly under the "Uniting for Peace" procedure evolved after the Korean War. At 2 A.M. on November 4, the Special Assembly adopted the Canadian resolution which requested the Secretary General to submit a plan within forty-eight hours for the setting up of an emergency international peace-keeping force to secure and supervise the cessation of hostilities.

Ironically, the U.N. Assembly met in a second emergency special session on the same Sunday, November 4, to consider the Soviet attack on Hungary. It will be recalled that the Hungarian Revolt broke out in Budapest on October 23 at the very time when the conspirators at Sèvres were completing their plans for the attack at Suez. Once hostilities had broken out in Egypt, the Russians were quick to take their advantage. Massive forces were brought into Hungary and the rebellion ruthlessly stamped out. Never in the history of NATO had the great alliance been in such disarray. While the United States and other partners were horrified that British and French forces were committed in the Middle East at a time of Soviet aggression in Eastern Europe,* the British and French for their part felt that the Red Army was so committed in Hungary and in the countries behind the Iron Curtain that they had their hands all the more free for action in the Middle East. It is clear that the developments at Suez bore heavily on those in Hungary. The Russians would have repressed the Hungarian revolt in any case; it was their good luck that the eyes of the world were blinking from the sands of Sinai.

By midnight of November 4 (a busy day in New York City) the Assembly had approved the Secretary General's first report and the Canadian General Burns, who had been commander of the truce-keeping forces in Palestine, was appointed as the U.N. Force Commander. Egypt formally accepted that the U.N. police force should take up positions in the Canal Zone. Canada, Norway, Colombia and other less committed nations offered to contribute troops to the proposed force. However, despite all the efforts at the U.N. that urgent Sunday, shortly after one o'clock on the morning of November 5, the news reached New York that British and French paratroops were being dropped on Port Said and at Port Fuad.

The architects of the limited war at Suez were still holding zealously to the plan of "Operation Musketeer," with the exception that, increasingly aghast at the explosion of world opinion against their enterprise, in London the British mana-

* Secretary of State Dulles in briefing President Eisenhower, November 1 said, "It is nothing less than tragic that at this very time, when we are on the point of winning an immense and long-hoped-for victory over Soviet colonialism in Eastern Europe, we should be forced to choose between following in the footsteps of Anglo-French colonialism in Asia and Africa, or splitting our course away from their course." [26]

gers of the affair wanted to push ahead on an expedited schedule. It was for this reason that the recently appointed new Minister of Defence, Anthony Head, flew hurriedly out to Cyprus to urge the Commander in Chief, General Keightley, to speed up the air-drop on Suez. Head urged in addition the need to avoid the bombardment of the civilian population and to modify the initial plan calling for the pursuit and destruction of Nasser, since it was by then obvious that this announced war objective had disastrously boomeranged.

Meanwhile, inexorably, the main amphibious force continued by sea from Malta, whence it had sortied on October 31 when the ultimatum against Egypt expired. It will be recalled that Malta is six days by convoy steaming from the beaches of Port Said and that the timetable worked out at Sèvres called for the troops to be landed no later than November 6, the magic date of the American presidential elections. Now, however, on Head's urging the paradrops at least were stepped up by one day and commenced on the 5th.

This was the day that Marshal Bulganin entered into vigorous diplomatic correspondence. He sent notes to Eden and Mollet referring to "the dangerous consequences of their aggressive war in Egypt." A similar minatory note was dispatched to Ben Gurion, while a letter in more general terms was also addressed to President Eisenhower. The notes to London and Paris clearly mentioned the threat of a possible Soviet atomic attack on these two capitals. Although after a telephone conversation Eden and Mollet agreed that they would not be intimidated by the Soviet threat, the British Government did send a signal to General Keightley on Cyprus that the possibility of Russian intervention by force could not be excluded. It was likewise reported that the Turkish Government had received a request from the U.S.S.R. for the passage through the Dardanelles of a Russian naval force consisting of a cruiser and three destroyers.

When at last the laggard force from Malta joined up with

the convoys from Cyprus on November 6, and a brief naval bombardment softened up the city for the amphibious landings at Port Said, time had just about run out of the glass for Sir Anthony Eden.

The Commonwealth was visibly shattering. Canada, the most faithful of the old dominions, was strenuously working to bring about a cease-fire through the skillful diplomacy of its Foreign Secretary, Lester Pearson; at the U.N. India and the Asian members east of Suez were vociferously against the British cause and even the support of Australia and New Zealand was muted. Within England itself, not only was the Labour opposition in screaming opposition, but fissures were developing within Eden's own Conservative Party. However, the conclusive influence on Eden — more massive than the frightening international run on the pound sterling or the vehement denunciations of Nehru, or the atomic threats of Bulganin — was the active opposition of President Eisenhower. Robert Murphy has summed it up best:

> Eden's greatest miscalculation was that he was unable to enlist the support of Eisenhower. . . . Nationwide elections in the United States were to be held the first Tuesday in November, Eisenhower, himself, was running for reelection, and he was confronted with the situation in which three friendly nations, two of them allies, had decided to wage war without a word of consultation with him. That alone would be sufficient explanation for his attitude. But Eisenhower's wrath went further than that. The President had made it clear that he thoroughly disapproved of what he regarded as 18th century tactics instead of recourse to diplomacy and United Nations procedures.[27]

Under these rising pressures, with the passage of resolutions adopted by the U.N. which afforded a way out, with the Israelis having ceased their hostilities and thus the pretext under which the expedition had been mounted, Eden came to the end of his rope. A Cabinet on November 6, that day to which so much significance had been ascribed, decided that a cease-fire must be entered into. Eden so informed Mollet. The French wanted to continue a series of paradrops on the theory that an additional twenty-four hours would insure the taking of the Canal Zone. In Pineau's judgment, since France had already been branded as an aggressor, they might as well complete the job, on the highly dubious assumption that by taking Suez, Nasser would be forced to flee. However, Eden was adamant and with reluctance the French Government had no option but to concur. At 4:34 P.M., Greenwich time, a telegram was sent from London to the Commander in Chief ordering the cease-fire for one minute before midnight, November 6 or approximately two in the morning, Cairo time, November 7.

6.

It is unnecessary here to pass in detail over subsequent clearing-up actions. In due course, the U.N. peace-keeping force of 6000 troops took over in the Canal Zone as the British and French forces were phased out. The U.N. undertook the massive job of clearing the Suez Canal, where the Egyptians had sunk twenty-seven ships and had destroyed two bridges into the channel of the Canal. Although the lengthy withdrawal afforded the Israelis time in which to make off with an immense haul of captured booty from the Sinai, nevertheless, the Gaza Strip was restored to U.N. supervision. A major Israeli gain, however, was the neutralization of the Straits of Tiran and the demolition under U.N. auspices of the Egyptian batteries at Sharm-El-Sheikh, thus opening the Gulf of Aqaba. Eventually, after arduous effort, the Canal was reopened and the first British ship was able to make a peaceful transit in August 1957. The Canal continued to be administered by the Egyptian authority, and in a memorandum dated March 18, 1957, the Government of the U.A.R. engaged itself to respect the spirit and letter of the Constantinople Convention. Tolls would continue to be paid to the Egyptian Canal Authority and a special fund would be set up for maintenance and improvement of the Canal. Claims resulting from nationalization would be subject to arbitration. In a note to the Secretary General of the United Nations dated April 24, 1957, the Foreign Minister of Egypt was able to say, "The Egyptian Government has the honor to state that the Suez Canal has returned to normal operation and, therefore, it can once more serve as a link between the nations of the world in the interest of peace and prosperity."

Later Eugene Black, President of the World Bank, worked out a settlement between the Egyptian Government and the Canal Company, incorporated in an accord signed at Rome on July 13, 1958, whereby the Company received an indemnity of almost 30 million Egyptian pounds to be paid in dollars and pounds sterling. Thus, the Suez episode was ended, but its lessons are still to be learned.

7.

As an example of how not to run a limited war the adventure at Suez was classic. In the first place, the British-French objectives were not only unrealizable but unrealistic. The first objective was to seize and operate the Suez Canal. This was immediately frustrated by Nasser's action in sinking block ships and bridges. Furthermore, the retention of the Canal Zone in hostile Arab territory would clearly have been an impossible exercise over the long run. The author well remembers attending a conference in London in 1952, when the question of evacuating the Suez Base was discussed between British and American diplomats, and where a paper by the Imperial Chiefs of Staff was tabled which stated as its premise that maintenance of a military base in hostile territory is in the long run impossible.

The second Anglo-French objective was the destruction of Nasser. However, even if he could conveniently be made to disappear, the British and French had no real alternative as a surrogate leader. Obviously, they thought to resuscitate and refurbish Naguib, who as one observer has pointed out, was perhaps the most guarded Egyptian in Egypt. Just how even a well-intentioned Naguib could rule against the united fury of his population, if set upon the throne as an Anglo-French puppet, is difficult to understand. Other candidates were canvassed, including the former Prime Minister, Ali Maher, whom a former British Ambassador in Cairo once described to the author as being "straight as a corkscrew." However, the political fact was starkly evident from the beginning that with Nasser destroyed, there could be no puppet ruler who could rule successfully for a day without the continued backing of foreign bayonets.

If the Anglo-French objectives were unattainable and unrealistic, the Israeli objectives were more calculatedly shrewd. As indicated early in this chapter, the Israeli war plan was constructed like an accordion, and the Israelis stood ready to profit by as much as they could grab under conditions of varying degrees of severity. Although militarily they mauled the Egyptians and retreated with a good haul of booty, and economically did in effect make open access to the Port of Elath on the Gulf of Aqaba, in a wider sense the Israelis lost. Their action brought on world deprecation and basic suspicion of the trustworthiness of Israeli motives and pretentions.

NATO and the British Commonwealth almost were destroyed. It was several years before relationships of confidence could painstakingly be rebuilt and reknit. It also became evident that NATO could not function without the wholehearted support of the United States.

The United Nations throughout played a valuable role in developing the issues and in providing the ports of exit for protagonists who wished or had to leave the stage. Once more the civilized smaller countries valiantly undertook the duty of stepping in to unscramble messes made by larger powers.

The Soviet Union gained significantly in world propaganda measurement by the spectacular threat of atomic bombing, set out in Marshal Bulganin's notes. It was not until two years later, when the American landing at Lebanon exploded the myth, that the Arabs, at least, were awakened from the conviction that in fact this threat of atomic reprisal bore a basic relationship to the British-French decision to back down. The most immediate gain for the U.S.S.R., however, was the unparalleled opportunity which the adventure at Suez offered them to stamp out an authentic "war of national liberation" in Hungary, while the world's attention was riveted on the Anglo-French-Israeli attack on Egypt.*

Nasser, of course, came off best. He emerged as the acknowledged leader of the Arabs with height and stature increased and with his own original objectives intact: the nationalization of the Suez Canal Company and operation of the Suez Canal by Egypt, and the new dam at Aswan, financed with Soviet money and built by Soviet and Egyptian engineers.

Nasser's deeply seated suspicions of "perfidious Albion" had only been more dramatically confirmed. The author remembers the nights of 1952 in his house in Zamalik at

---

* The author was in New Delhi at the time, as a delegate to the UNESCO General Conference, and well remembers the ink-eradicator effect on the headlines from Hungary imposed by the headlines from Suez.

Cairo when Nasser and his inevitable companion, the silent Hakim Amer, used to come to the terrace and discuss their objectives for the reform of Egypt. The profundity of Nasser's hatred and suspicion of the British was even then apparent and nothing that could be urged in favor of a more objective sizing-up of British intentions had any effect on Nasser.

Now with the attack on Suez, Nasser was only more convinced of British imperial duplicity. This explains his active policy toward Cyprus and his fixed intent of doing everything possible to winkle the British out of their bases on that island. After all, the airdrop and bombardment at Suez were based on the island where more than Venus was born. This distrust of the British likewise explains Nasser's adventures in Yemen and the presence in that medieval country of fifty thousand Egyptian troops. Nasser's ultimate strategic aim is to see the British out of Aden; to remove what he conceives to be an Anglo-Saxon pincers around the Arab world.

The influence of the United States and its President Eisenhower was never more gigantically evident than in the affair of Suez. Perhaps the most cynical and disastrous miscalculation of all was the foolish preoccupation of the Israelis, British and French over the date of the presidential elections. Eisenhower cared nothing at all for the presumed connection between his desire to be reelected and the line of policy which he saw crystal-clear as to what should be done with regard to America's allies who had undertaken to violate the U.N. Charter.

Thus the episode at Suez ended. In the next chapter there can be studied another exercise in limited war in the Near East, which came to a happier and more constructive conclusion.

CHAPTER VII

The American Landing in Lebanon, 1958 *

1.

AFTER THE ADVENTURE at Suez there was a power vacuum in the Near East. Clearly, Nasser was in the ascendancy as an authentic Arab hero. Temporarily, at least, the luster of Israeli military prowess was tarnished by the general condemnation of world opinion. Meanwhile, the Soviet Union busily sought to obtain advantage of the situation. Its engineers swarmed over the new Aswan Dam; its technicians trained Arab armies in the use of Soviet weapons; and, in general, the Red Star moved toward zenith.[1]

There were, of course, other Arab leaders whose ambitions and goals were opposite to those of the Rais of Egypt. Foremost of these was Nuri Pasha, the tough, Turkish-trained and durable elder statesman of Iraq. The weak but wily King Saud of Saudi Arabia, the young, inexperienced but courageous monarch of Jordan, King Hussein, and the Christian President of Lebanon, Camille Chamoun, were each in varying degree and for different reasons opponents of Nasser.

In the power vacuum then existing in the Near East the United States sought to develop at least a countervailing force. However, the attempts of the Department of State to secure Arab support for the principles of the Middle East

* This is an eyewitness account. "The American Ambassador" cited herein was the author.

Joint Resolution — otherwise known as the Eisenhower Doctrine — met with scant success. In fact, only one country — Lebanon — joined on March 16, 1957, in a communiqué endorsing the principles of this doctrine, which provided simply that the United States would come to the assistance of any country in the Middle East which was threatened by the attack of a Communist power.

It is against this background that the American landing in Lebanon on July 15, 1958 should be judged.

On October 25, 1958, the last of the American forces which had landed in Lebanon voluntarily departed. It is now possible to evaluate this exercise in the diplomacy of force and to draw certain conclusions from the experience of a joint diplomatic and military enterprise. Although no guns were fired in anger and no casualties were inflicted upon the indigenous population, this was, in fact, an exercise in limited war. The objectives which were achieved were not only in the interest of Lebanon and of the United States, but also of the world through the maintenance of peace in the Near East.

Before considering the actual history of the American landing in Lebanon, it is first essential to have some background as to what happened in the summer of 1958 before the American forces eventually intervened at the city of Beirut.

The Secretary of State, in conversation with an Allied ambassador in Washington, summarized the Lebanese crisis succinctly when he said that the insurrection in Lebanon was made up of two factors: outside intervention, plus the internal problem of whether or not President Chamoun would, or should, succeed himself in office for a second term.

On this latter aspect of the problem, the Lebanese constitution forbids a president's immediately succeeding himself for a second six-year term of office. In consequence, had the outgoing president decided to stand for reelection in the summer of 1958, it would have required a constitutional amendment, which can be voted by a two-thirds majority of the Lebanese Parliament. As for popular opinion on the much discussed issue of whether President Camille Chamoun should attempt such an amendment of the constitution as a prerequisite to reelection, the country was almost evenly divided, with a large proportion of the Moslem population opposed and an equal number of the Christian population in favor. This broad division of opinion was infinitely subdivided, but for the purposes of this study it is not necessary to go into greater detail. From the aspect of the diplomatic problem, however, it should be mentioned that many of the Moslems who opposed the President were strong Arab nationalists, and were embittered at President Chamoun's having espoused the Eisenhower Doctrine, as well as having earlier refused to sever relations with Great Britain and France following the episode at Suez in 1956. As for the proponents of President Chamoun, it was important to note that the influential Lebanese emigrés colonies in the Western Hemisphere were wholly for the President, and that a variety of governments friendly to the United States, including Turkey, Iraq, Iran, and Jordan, felt that President Chamoun merited support.

2.

On May 8, 1958, a left-wing editor of the Beirut newspaper *Telegraph* was murdered by unknown assailants. Rioting broke out in the city of Tripoli on the next day. This was Lebanon's second largest center of population, with a Moslem majority much opposed to the prospect of a second term for President Chamoun. During the next few days, the street fighting in Tripoli grew more severe with mounting casualties, and in the capital of Beirut a general strike was declared in the Moslem quarter, called the Basta. Already it was evident that the insurgents were receiving help from outside Lebanon, principally in the form of funds, with a considerable incursion of clandestine arms. There was also a violent campaign of denunciation of President Chamoun by the Damascus and Cairo radios and press — one more instance of what this writer has called "audio-visual aggression."

Although the insurrection was but three days old, already on May 11 President Chamoun commented to the American Ambassador on the remark of his Foreign Minister, Dr. Malik, that the government of Lebanon should begin to think tentatively of asking the United States for the landing of a division of Marines. Two days later, as the revolution spread and the central government increasingly lost control over the internal security situation, the beleaguered President summoned the ambassadors of the United States, the United Kingdom and France. He indicated that his strife-torn country might have to ask for military assistance from the three friendly powers.

The American Government was convinced from evidence at hand that there had, in fact, been serious outside intervention in the Lebanese civil war coming from the United Arab Republic. It also felt that the maintenance of the independence of a small free country such as Lebanon was important if world peace were to be maintained, and if the integrity of other states were not to be violated with impunity. In consequence, on May 14, the American Ambassador was authorized to inform the Lebanese President that although Lebanon should not invoke American assistance unless its integrity were generally threatened and its own forces were not sufficient for the protection of the state, nevertheless the United States was prepared, upon request both from the President and the government of Lebanon, to send certain combat forces which would have the dual mission of protecting American life and property and of assisting the government of Lebanon in its military program for the preservation of the integrity and independence of the Republic. At the same time, the United States would expect that Lebanon would file a complaint with the United Nations Security Council against external interference in its internal affairs; that at least some Arab states would be prepared publicly to support Lebanon in its appeal for aid; and, finally, that if the United States assisted it would not be on the issue of the internal question of the Lebanese presidential election.

As for the United Kingdom and France, they had already, in 1956, by secret notes given assurances to Lebanon of their readiness to preserve the integrity of the Republic. In consequence, the only new blank check which President Chamoun desired to draw was that of the United States.

It is interesting, in view of later declarations on this point, that the Department of State did not consider under the circumstances of the moment that U.S. intervention would fall within the provisions of Section II of the Joint Resolution on the Middle East, the so-called Eisenhower Doctrine. *

3.

The civil war in Lebanon rapidly assumed the proportions of an armed stalemate. The rebels controlled most of the

---

* So read the instructions received by the author on May 14, 1958, in the Department's telegram 4271, May 13, which outlined the conditions laid down to President Chamoun. Probably President Eisenhower in Chapter XI, p. 271, of his recent memoirs, *Waging Peace*, in which he indicated that "Our intervention would be a response to a proper request from a legally constituted government and in accordance with the principles stated in the Middle East Doctrine," had in mind the basic confrontation of Soviet versus Western power in the Middle Eastern vacuum, and the essence of the Doctrine, which is, "the United States regards as vital to the national interest and world peace the preservation of the independence and integrity of the nations of the Middle East." The text of the Joint Resolution goes on to authorize the use of American "armed forces to assist any nation or group of such nations requesting assistance against armed aggression from any country controlled by international communism." In 1958 the United States did not claim that the U.A.R. — Syria and Egypt — from which the aggression against Lebanon undeniably came, was controlled by international Communism.

Moslem city of Tripoli in the north, much of the Moslem
town of Saida in the south, the Moslem center of Beirut, and
large areas in the Bekaa Yalley contiguous with Syria, and in
the mountainous central region of the Chouf, where the
Druzes of Kamal Jumblat had been reinforced by a band
of six hundred fellow tribesmen from Syria.

The daily pay of the insurgent forces came by various
subterranean channels from the United Arab Republic, then
joined in Egypt and Syria. There probably were at maximum
between five and seven thousand armed men on the insurgent side, with a small but significant cadre in Tripoli,
Beirut, and, to a lesser degree, the Chouf made up of noncoms and a few officers from Syria. However, the bulk of the
fighting forces on the rebel side were Lebanese. Some were
imbued with a definite political fixation against the supposed
intent of President Chamoun to succeed himself; others were
out for whatever advantage, pecuniary or otherwise, they
might stand to pick up. For example, when an American
television correspondent interviewed an insurgent and asked
why he was fighting, the Arabic interpreter replied for the
man in English, "I am fighting for liberty and against tyr-
anny." But actually, what the trooper had said in Arabic was
more brief — "I am fighting for money."

On the government side there were civilian partisans of
President Chamoun, armed from a variety of sources, while
the regularly constituted armed forces of the state, consisting of the army and the gendarmerie, intervened largely
for the purpose of keeping open certain essential lines of
communication, or of preventing rebel sorties from their
strongholds in Tripoli, the Basta and the Chouf, but without
at the same time making any determined endeavor to crush
the rebellion.

The Lebanese Army was but a reflection of the population
mosaic of the country, made up almost equally of Christian
and Moslem troops. The Commander in Chief, General Fuad

Chehab, feared that if he ordered his forces to destroy the rebel strongholds, his army might divide on a strictly Moslem versus Christian axis, with the result that the country would then be plunged into a bloody confessional conflict, with forces on both sides possessed of ample weapons and the necessary military techniques and discipline mutually to destroy each other.

The upshot of this uneasy military balance was by midsummer a stalemate, with much of the area of Lebanon in rebel control, but with the government forces maintaining open both longitudinal and lateral lines of communication, as well as free access to the port and airport of Beirut. In the capital a dusk-to-dawn curfew prevailed and many people tired of each other, and of playing bridge.

With the contingent assurances of military support from the Western powers under the conditions which had been outlined to the President, joint planning was begun by the British and American military on a standby basis in the event that the President and government of Lebanon should call for Allied assistance. Also, at this time a new command was set up for the first time in American history called a Specified Command, later to be known as CINCSPECOME, or Commander in Chief, Specified Command, Middle East. CINCSPECOME was entrusted to the experienced hands of Admiral James L. Holloway, Jr., who already wore the hat of CINCNELM,* based in London.

On June 6 the Lebanese Foreign Minister lodged before the U.N. Security Council an official complaint of interference in the internal affairs of Lebanon by the United Arab Republic. On June 11, the Security Council voted to send observers to Lebanon and the first of these neutral officers arrived the next day. The rapidly expanded U.N. Observer

---

* CINCNELM: Commander in Chief, Naval Forces, Eastern Atlantic and Mediterranean.

Group, dubbed UNOGIL, was unarmed and initially much limited in terms of transport, although eventually it did acquire light observation planes and helicopters. Since, as has been indicated above, most of the country was already in rebel hands, these unarmed observers were confined largely to the few principal highways still kept open by the Lebanese security forces. In consequence, their reports to the Secretary General of the United Nations revealed little to substantiate the claim of the Lebanese Government of "massive" military intervention from Syria.* By lodging its complaint with the Security Council, however, the Lebanese Government had already fulfilled one of the conditions precedent to possible Allied military intervention, if that government should so request.

One other of the conditions laid down when the American Ambassador, on May 14, had communicated his government's readiness to consider assistance to the Lebanese Government was that an appeal for help to maintain the integrity of the Republic must emanate not only from the President, but likewise from the government of Lebanon. Here again this condition was placed in readiness to be met. On June 16, the Lebanese Cabinet unanimously voted full powers to the President to call for the military assistance of friendly powers if, in his judgment, he felt the integrity of the state could be saved by no other means.

As for the third condition, that the government of Lebanon have the support of at least some other Arab governments, this was readily and even urgently forthcoming from the government of Iraq and from the government of the Kingdom of Jordan.

* The three U.N. observers, an ex-President of Ecuador, Señor Galo Plaza, an Ambassador, Rajeswar Dayal of India, and a Norwegian Air Force General named Odd Bull, once had themselves photographed on the porch of the author's beach cabin at Beirut in the posture of the three monkeys of Nikko.

As for the issue of the presidential elections, President Chamoun had many times declared confidentially to the American Ambassador that this was no longer an issue; his only concern was for the preservation of the integrity and independence of the state. However, for reasons of stubbornness or pride he failed to make a statement to the Lebanese people.

Thus, by mid-June, one month after the President of Lebanon had placed the three friendly Western powers on notice that he might find himself compelled to ask for military intervention, the conditions precedent to such a step had, so far as the government of Lebanon was concerned, been fulfilled. So far as the American government was involved, however, there was deep concern lest the United States be asked to intervene in a situation where, in effect, the arrival of our forces would be construed as intervention in a purely internal conflict centered upon a struggle for continuance in office. There was likewise no desire in Washington to see American troops deployed on the beaches of Beirut if the Lebanese armed forces might resist an American or an Allied landing. On several occasions these apprehensions were made known not only to President Chamoun, but to the Lebanese Commander in Chief, General Chehab. The General warned the Ambassador that if U.S. troops did land, his own might get out of hand — at least to the extent of not saving Chamoun.

4.

The situation radically changed on July 14, 1958. What had heretofore concerned only an internal struggle in Lebanon, abetted by outside intervention, became but one aspect of a wider crisis affecting the entire Near East. On the morning of July 14 the government of Nuri Said and the royal family of Iraq were destroyed by a coup d'état under the leadership of Brigadier Abdel Karim Kassim. Washington had very reliable information that a similar coup d'état had been scheduled against King Hussein of Jordan for July 17. In consequence, when on the morning of July 14, President Chamoun separately summoned the chiefs of mission of the United States, the United Kingdom, and France, his appeal for instant military intervention was reflected against a much broader background, namely, the map of the Near East.

President Chamoun asked for American intervention within forty-eight hours on the mistaken intelligence, derived from newspapers, that the Sixth Fleet was largely deployed on the coasts of Spain and could not reach the Levant in a shorter time. His requests of the British Chargé and the French Ambassador were for aid within twenty-four hours. By arrangement between the powers concerned, however, it was decided that only American forces would land in Lebanon; the British were to respond to a similar appeal from the government of Jordan. Ultimately, the French desire for a "token" participation was skillfully met with no untoward repercussions when on July 17 the French cruiser *De Grasse*, wearing the flag of Vice Admiral Jozan, with escorting destroyers, called at Beirut and departed during the night.

President Chamoun's request for American military intervention was met with extreme celerity by the U.S. government. Far from landing within the space of forty-eight hours, the American Ambassador was empowered to inform the President that U.S. Marines would commence their disembarkation at Beirut at 1500 hours, local time, July 15. The Ambassador was instructed to add that the United States would expect "full co-operation from the Lebanese armed forces."

When the Ambassador imparted this information to President Chamoun the latter asked the American diplomat to convey the tidings to the Commander in Chief, General Chehab. The President later asked the Ambassador to postpone his call on the Commander in Chief from noon to 1:30, obviously in the hope of forestalling an Army coup d'état before the American forces had landed.

In fact, it was not until the Ambassador called on General Chehab that the Commander in Chief clearly understood that the United States intended to land a battalion of Marines in the instant. As the Ambassador was speaking to the General, his Chief of Staff burst in to announce at a quarter to two that seven vessels were standing by six miles off the airport. General Chehab told the Ambassador that they were on the brink of disaster, and asked if the American troops at least could stay on board their ships, which then might enter the port. However, an attempt to make contact with the local American commanders was fruitless, and the Marines landed and secured the airport ahead of schedule. As of 6:00 P.M. the landing had been accomplished, the airport re-opened to commercial traffic, and Lebanese troops returned to normal guard duty at the airport. Beirut in general was quiet, although there was some rifle fire from the Christian quarter where those elements were rejoicing.

Scarcely had the Ambassador returned from his afternoon call on the Commander in Chief than the head of Chamoun's private army, Deputy Naim Moghabghab, came breathlessly to the Chancery to say that Chamoun had word that Chehab intended to arrest him and that the coup d'état was scheduled for 3:00 P.M. This was ten minutes away. Chamoun himself telephoned the Ambassador by secret voice radio asking to "send Marines with tanks quickly." However, since the time was so tight, although the Ambassador did send messages to the local American commanders (again to no avail although the communications were, in fact, received), he decided, as an ultimate recourse, to telephone General

Chehab. The General said he feared an army coup d'état but had sought to dissuade his officers. His hand would be strengthened if the Americans could delay their landing. The Ambassador replied that the American forces were landing in aid of the legitimate government of Lebanon and if the Army should arrest the Chief of State there would be "most disagreeable consequences." After a long pause, General Chehab said he would "recommend" to his officers that the coup against Chamoun be stayed.

The first day of the landing drew to a close with a visit to the Ambassador by the senior American officer present, a naval captain who had been in charge of the APA's and AKA's which had brought the initial landing force. This was the captain who, when importuned by the Embassy on voice radio to give some heed to the suggestions of General Chehab, had answered that he was subject to the orders of the Commander of the Sixth Fleet, who was under the instructions of CINCNELM, who in turn was responsible to the Chief of Naval Operations, who in his turn was under the direction of the President of the United States. This sort of brass-bound answer torn from the naval regulations did not exactly fit the needs of an emergency situation. The naval captain furthermore suggested that, if the Ambassador wanted to see him, he could fly out to his flagship. The upshot of this bureaucratic exchange was a very firm indication by the Ambassador that he would receive the "Commodore" at his residence and very quickly. The captain did arrive, puffing, accepted a large bourbon and soda, and said, "Ambassador, by our landing today we have prevented an economic depression in the United States!"

Similar lack of coordination was experienced when the Embassy sought to give an affirmative expression to President Chamoun's desperate appeal for help by secret radio when he personally asked the Ambassador to "send Marines quickly with tanks." The Ambassador sent his Air Attaché and an Arabic-speaking officer to the Beirut airport, which was in the hands of the Marines, but found that the senior officer present, a lieutenant colonel, was so rigidly bound by his mimeographed orders that he could not venture from the immediate defense perimeter of the airport. Had, in fact, Chamoun been killed while the Marines had "landed and had the situation in hand," the resultant picture would not have been flattering to the Marines or to the over-all effort of the United States in seeking to help the legally constituted Chief of State of Lebanon.

5.

On the next day real disaster was averted by a hair's breadth.

Early on the morning of July 16 the Ambassador received a visit from Lieutenant Colonel Hadd, USMC, who had been the senior officer present at the airport on the preceding day. He was accompanied by Brigadier General Sidney Wade, USMC, who had landed on the morning of the sixteenth and had assumed command of the Marines then on the beach in the vicinity of the airport. The Ambassador thereupon took General Wade to call on President Chamoun, emphasizing the near-miss of the preceding afternoon when the President had called for Marine assistance which could not be furnished because of the extreme rigidity of the orders under which the Marines on the beach were operating. General Wade indicated that he too was under an imperative necessity by his instructions to commence prompt deployment from the airport into Beirut where he was to occupy the port area — the same area to which General Chehab had invited them to come, unopposed, in their own ships.

Subsequent to this visit to President Chamoun, the Embassy learned that important elements of the Lebanese artillery and armored force were being deployed along the airport road as if to meet the advancing column of Marines. Upon receiving this intelligence, the Ambassador asked General Wade if he could not delay his entry into Beirut at least until the Lebanese guns could be pointed in some other direction. General Wade hesitated because he said his orders were explicit, but at last agreed to defer his deployment until 10:00 A.M. This left roughly one hour in which the Embassy could operate.

At this juncture President Chamoun telephoned the Ambassador to say that he was closeted with General Chehab and asked if the Ambassador could join this conference. The Ambassador at the palace told the President and Commander in Chief of the disquieting disposition of the Lebanese guns and invited General Chehab at once to accompany him out to the airport road to see what could be done about a menacing situation. With some hesitation but with the active urging of the President, the Commander in Chief then accompanied the Ambassador in the Embassy official car out to the guns. Here they found that all the available Lebanese artillery and tanks, ranging in fire power from 105's to 75 mm. recoilless rifles, had been deployed in echelon along the airport highway and on feeder roads, thus providing angle fire. The Marine column had meanwhile approached from the airport and was halted in single file facing the Lebanese tanks and artillery with an interval of about one hundred yards between the two forces.

As General Chehab and the Ambassador got out of their car, by great good fortune the Supreme U.S. Commander, Admiral James Holloway, arrived by the car of the Naval Attaché, the Admiral having just arrived at the Beirut airport by helicopter from his flagship. He was accompanied by Task Force Commander, Rear Admiral Howard A. Yaeger, and contact was soon established with the senior Marine commander, General Wade, and Lieutenant Colonel Hadd. The Ambassador introduced the two Commanders in Chief and General Chehab suggested that the party repair to the nearby Lebanese Army Combat School where he would have telephonic communications with headquarters.

There ensued a long conversation in Arabic between General Chehab and his Chief of Staff, Colonel Salaam, who was at the Defense Ministry. There were nearby bursts of machinegun fire which General Chehab said came from rebel forces, although the suspicion occurred to the Ambassador and Admiral Holloway that this fire might have come from the Lebanese troops in order to justify the General's professed concern that the Marine column should not advance until this pocket of "rebel resistance" had been wiped out.

As the upshot of a long exchange between the American side and the Lebanese Commander in Chief, plus General Chehab's instructions to his General Staff, it was at last agreed that the Marine column should proceed slowly into the port area of Beirut, each three vehicles, whether tanks or personnel carriers, to be separated from the other unit of three vehicles by a Lebanese Army escort jeep.

Under this arrangement the first units of the Marine column began slowly to deploy toward Beirut along the coastal highway, and the Ambassador suggested to General Chehab that if all seemed to be going well the General might wish to join his own car and return to Beirut. This General Chehab did; however, it soon became apparent that the arrangement of sending the Marine column into the city in sausage-link array had fallen down as the supposed Lebanese Army escort jeeps did not materialize. In consequence, Admiral Holloway decided to move the entire column in as originally planned since by this time the Lebanese artillery and tanks had received orders not to fire. Although it was not known at that time, apparently the Lebanese Air Force, which had been orbiting overhead, likewise had been instructed by its commander to open fire on the Marine column. This order was later countermanded by instruction from General Headquarters.

Most of a very hot afternoon was then spent by Admirals Holloway and Yaeger operating from the Ambassador's car in shepherding the Marine tanks and personnel carriers down the coastal highway and into the port area of Beirut. At one time the Ambassador was able to dart into the Embassy chancery, give instructions for the protocol visits which he proposed to make with Admiral Holloway, decant his poodle dog, and embark a stenographer who took dictation of a telegram describing the morning's events as the official column, led by the Admiral and the Ambassador, slowly moved into Beirut. Ultimately, the Marines were placed in possession of the port area and the flagships of CINCSPECOME were brought alongside. Calls were made by the Admiral and Ambassador on President Chamoun, Prime Minister Solh, and — at Jounieh, General Chehab's residence — the Commander in Chief. Luncheon was served very late at the Embassy residence on July 16.

However, as the result of an arduous day's work, the possibility of a Lebanese Army mutiny and consequent attack on the American landing forces had been averted, and by the end of the day General Chehab told Admiral Holloway and the Ambassador that "this day marks an historic occasion in the history of Lebanese-American military cooperation" — something of a euphemism for a Commanding General whose troops had almost precipitated a military attack on the forces of the United States — and for an American Commander in Chief whose troops had thus gained the hard way the objective whose unimpeded attainment they had rejected.

Although it was subsequently ascertained that the Lebanese units had local orders to fire on the Marines, this was not an instruction from the Commander in Chief or, above all, the Lebanese President and Government, who had requested friendly U.S. intervention. The deployment of the Lebanese armor and tanks in this threatening attitude had been the insubordinate act of certain younger officers in the armor and artillery. The impact of this act of insubordination on the political aspects of the American landing might well have jeopardized the objectives for which both the diplomats and the military were working.

6.

It is a credit to the command on both sides that, despite this near miss, very cordial and effective working relationships were promptly established between Admiral Holloway and General Chehab, and throughout the lower echelons in the American and Lebanese command structure. In fact, by the very evening of July 16, military patrols composed of Lebanese and American units were jointly operating on the streets of Beirut.

Although the Marine Corps beach deployment was the first of the American landings in Lebanon, an equally important military role was assigned to units of the 24th Airborne Brigade, under command of Brigadier General David Gray, U.S. Army, and eventually to an entire battalion of tanks which had been deployed from Germany. The over-all military command of land forces was in the hands of Major General Paul Adams, U.S. Army, who relieved Brigadier General Wade, U.S. Marine Corps, on July 26. The total number of American forces eventually deployed in the vicinity of Beirut came close to 15,000, of which 8000 were U.S. Army, and about 6000 Marines. Full credit is likewise due to the U.S. Air Force, whose planes transported the units of the 24th Airborne Brigade, and elements of whose 19th Air Force carried out their missions successfully.

The U.S. Navy in the Sixth Fleet, with ancillary elements brought from elsewhere as required, did a magnificent job in supplying the logistic requirements of the troops onshore. In fact, to the Arab observer, the seemingly effortless ease with which so important an operation was conducted, and the smooth synchronization of the three military elements of air, land, and sea power which was maintained gave dramatic proof, not only of the determination of the United States to fulfill its political objectives, but of the highly disciplined means it used to achieve these ends.

A fourth element lay in the diplomatic arm. It is quite possible that the landing would have been opposed, and the course of events had a different outcome, had not the American Embassy been fully conversant with what was going on, and had it not intervened at the critical time to prevent untoward events from coming to pass. On a continuing basis the confident relationship which was instantly established between Admiral Holloway, as CINCSPECOME, and General Adams, as Commander of the land forces, with the American Ambassador and his staff made possible a smooth day-by-day direction of the American military presence in Lebanon. So confident and complete was this relationship among the higher echelons of official Americans operating in Lebanon that at no time was there any difference of opinion between the Ambassador and the Commander in Chief. There was, therefore, no necessity to invoke the paragraph of the joint Defense-State directive to the Commander in Chief, which stated, "In case of difference between the military commander and the local United States diplomatic representative in regard to political matters relating exclusively to Lebanon, the views of the latter shall be controlling."

Tribute should here be paid to the influence and diplomatic skill of the American Under Secretary of State for Political Affairs, Mr. Robert Murphy, who was dispatched July 16 to Beirut by President Eisenhower as his personal representative. Thus there was a high-powered "diplomatic landing" in Lebanon coincident with the military landing. Secretary Murphy's long days and nights of patient conversation on both sides of the barricades did much in helping the Lebanese to arrive at constitutional elections and the orderly ending of President Chamoun's legitimate term of office.

The American landing in Lebanon and the British air envelopment in Jordan were undoubtedly decisive in preventing the wiping out of the Lebanese and Jordanian governments by force in a manner similar to that of the Iraqi government in Baghdad. In consequence, it can be fairly said that this limited use of force was successful in achieving the political objective, which was to maintain peace in the Middle East and to show the world generally that the United States and Great Britain, with the support of their allies, were ready to go to great effort and risk to assist small, free, friendly nations to maintain their integrity and independence.

7.

Scarcely had the Marine amtracs hit the beach and the Air Force Hercules transports landed their troops, weapons, and cargo at the airport than Admiral Holloway and the Ambassador in Beirut, and the Defense and State Departments in Washington, began to plan for the withdrawal of the American forces from Lebanon.

One of the greatest concerns which had haunted both the diplomatic and military officers in responsible positions was the possibility that once our forces were landed in the Near East they might be compelled indefinitely to remain. The past history of military incursions into the Levant since the time of Alexander the Great gave ample reason to sustain such an apprehension. In fact, in the entire history of Phoenicia, which goes back some five thousand years, no foreign invading army had ever come by invitation of the inhabitants, or had left voluntarily without causing casualties.

As the security situation in Lebanon became stabilized, it was possible for the Lebanese Parliament to meet in plenary session, deputies both of the rebel and of the loyalist factions voting for a new president. The Commander in Chief of the Armed Forces, General Fuad Chehab, received the necessary two-thirds majority and was elected on July 31. On the same day the U.S. Secretary of State announced that U.S. forces would be withdrawn from Lebanon as soon as the Lebanese Government requested their removal. The President-elect, in his first message to the Lebanese people, stated that foremost among national objectives was the withdrawal of foreign troops. In consequence, there was agreement in principle on both sides, Lebanese and American, that our forces should leave as soon as possible. General Chehab himself, however, indicated that he would not request withdrawal until the security situation had improved.

From the diplomatic point of view it seemed essential that the initiative for withdrawal should remain in American hands. Nationalistic Arab radio and press attacks could not in that case successfully allege that the American landing was an exercise in imperialism. As a matter of fact, if the Americans kept the initiative, they would prove to the world that this was a case of "imperialism in reverse."

Even before the new president took office on September 23 the phased withdrawal of the American forces had begun. The 2nd Marine Battalion left in late August, and it was agreed between General Chehab and Admiral Holloway that two additional Marine battalions could be removed by mid-September. Ultimately the United States unilaterally announced on October 8 its intention to withdraw all forces from Lebanon by the end of that month. Thus, officially and on the record, the withdrawal of American forces was at American initiative. It was, in fact, a very considerable diplomatic success thus to have carried out a massive military operation and to have removed the troops unilaterally, although in close and cordial agreement with the Lebanese Government.

While these politico-military developments were in progress, a peaceful transition took place when President Camille Chamoun served out his constitutional term of office and handed over his duties to General Chehab, the new president, on September 23. It should not be thought, however, that everything went smooth as silk in the Embassy/ CINCSPECOME relations with certain elements of the Lebanese population. For example, it had been widely believed by the more militant Christian faction that the sole purpose of the American landing was to wipe out the Moslem opposition by a classic bombardment of the Basta in Beirut. The Lebanese, throughout the nineteenth century and later, had become used to armed intervention by foreign powers, and to naval bombardment as a means of conducting foreign policy. Some Lebanese could not see why the Americans had troubled to land at Beirut if they did not use their firepower against the rebels. The Americans had wider ranges in sight, however, and more important targets at which to aim. To have landed troops to engage in partisan fighting to sustain one faction against the other would have been an unwise act; while to kill Moslems on behalf of Christians would have inflamed the 44,000,000 Arab Moslems and their co-religionists as far as the South China Sea.

8.

While the American forces exerted a static influence in Lebanon after the change in administration between Cha-

moun and Chehab, the insurrection took a new turn and
reached a new pitch of intensity. On September 19 a journal-
ist of the militant Christian Phalange Party was kidnaped
and murdered, following torture, because of an article he had
written reviling President Nasser of the United Arab Republic. In reprisal, the Phalange called for a general strike of
Christians, which was promptly carried out. Since the principal business and financial enterprises of Beirut were in
Christian hands, the economic impact of this general strike
was far more paralyzing to Lebanon than the more protracted, but less effective, general strike which had been imposed by the Moslem rebels since the outbreak of hostilities.

It was thus in a tense and ominous atmosphere that President Chehab was inaugurated on September 23. His first
appointment of a cabinet headed by one of the rebel leaders,
Rachid Karame, who had led the insurrection in Tripoli,
brought an outcry from the Christian half of the Lebanese
population. The ex-president, Chamoun, who had withdrawn to a retreat in the mountains, found himself the focus
of an almost ecstatic mob of partisans howling for action
against the new government. In other words, the impasse, if
it could be called such, had grown more serious, and the task
of reconciliation more difficult.

As the crisis wore on, there were two armed camps in
Beirut, the Moslem Basta and the Christian Casbah, with
the Lebanese Army and the American forces on the outskirts
of Beirut and in the port area maintaining an uneasy stalemate between the two.

In this situation, at the suggestion of President Chehab
and his Foreign Minister, Philipe Takla, and at the request
of the leader of the Christian Phalange, Sheikh Pierre Gemayel, the American Ambassador undertook mediatory conversations between the various warring factions. Because the
highways out of Beirut were barricaded with the living bod-

ies of Phalangist women, he resorted to U.S. Army helicopter in flying between Beirut, the mountain abode of Chamoun and the small port town of Junieh where President Chehab resided. As his official report to Washington indicated, on October 10, five days before the final solution was found, "The Ambassador that day saw former President Bechara El-Khoury at five in the afternoon, President Chehab at six, [rebel leader] Saeb Salaam at nine, Gemayel at ten, and President Chehab once more at eleven o'clock that evening, still seeking to work out a formula which would permit a viable solution to emerge. At the end of a very long day, President Chehab correctly described the situation by saying that both sides were now so groggy with fatigue they would eventually stumble to some sort of live-and-let-live solution."

Ultimately, thanks to leadership on both sides, with the patient and constant statesmanship of President Chehab exercising a continuous pressure, an agreement was reached on the formula proposed by the Phalangist leader, Sheikh Pierre Gemayel, of a solution of "no victor, no vanquished." Thus, when the country had almost reached the brink of dissolution, the innate good sense of the Lebanese began to prevail and on October 15 the civil war ended with the establishment of a four-man cabinet which epitomized the formula of "no victor, no vanquished." This government, which was to endure for another year of fruitful and constructive activity, was composed of Rachid Karame and Haj Hussein Oueini on the Moslem side, and Pierre Gemayel and Raymond Edde representing the Christian half of Lebanon.

9.

Perhaps rarely in the history of war have foreign troops shown more excellent deportment in a strange land. The exemplary discipline manifested by the American troops,

both Army and Marine, was a source of wonderment throughout the Arab world. In light of the previous experience that
Arabs had had with foreign armies, such forbearance on the
part of invading forces was completely without precedent.
In fact, the real hero of the American landing in Lebanon
was the U.S. GI, whether he wore a uniform of blue, khaki
or green.

As a result of this exercise in military and diplomatic cooperation, certain tangible effects in the interest of the
United States were achieved. In the first place, the integrity
and independence of a small free Arab nation were maintained against external aggression. The United States, by its
intervention, made clear to all the world that it stood by its
friends, irrespective of their size. It is also indubitable that,
without the static presence of American forces in Lebanon,
the crisis would have continued and the constructive elements in the country, which ultimately were able to carry out
presidential elections and to find a solution, could not have
achieved their purpose.

Of greater politically strategic importance was the fact
that the American intervention in Lebanon destroyed the
myth in Arab eyes of Soviet invincibility. Following the
Suez crisis in 1956, Soviet propaganda had succeeded in convincing many of the credulous in the Arab world that it was
the U.S.S.R.'s threat of atomic reprisal on London and Paris
which had caused the withdrawal of the French and British
forces from Egypt. Now, however, when the chips were
down and an American expeditionary force, at Lebanese request, had landed on the coast of the Arab world, Khrushchev was nowhere to be found.

This American action left indelible impressions in Arab
minds. The Americans were mighty but they kept their
might in check. They came faithfully when called by a
friend but they left without harming him. The old "imperi-

alists" had not acted like this. This was an inverse imperialism, if indeed imperialism was the word for the occasion. And so the tale ran, not only in the souks and the bazaars and the coffee houses, but in the villas of the statesmen and in the map rooms of the General Staffs. The word ran also to the New Nations, the Uncommitted Countries fiercely determined to preserve their newly won sovereignty against all comers.

So much for the basic results of the American landing in Lebanon in 1958. As for the specific conclusions which may be drawn from this study in diplomatic and military cooperation, the three main points are:

(1) There was need for the capability of high-level, flexible, over-all command decision as of zero hour, D-Day, and not D-Day plus two. Even if the Commander in Chief himself could not have been present, there was a requirement for greater leeway in adjusting previously written orders to changing local situations; nor should what limited power of command decision there was have been left to a lieutenant colonel on shore and a naval captain at sea whose only recourse was the rule book. Even a one-star Marine general thought his orders so peremptory as not to permit delay of execution beyond one hour — an hour plus execution which might have proved fatal to the whole purpose of the landing. The orders for the initial phase of the landing were too rigid. In fixing upon quite reasonable military objectives, they left no room for the imagination. And imagination in war is one of the ingredients which go into the making of great commanders.

(2) In the command vacuum of the first two days of the landing, the gap had to be bridged by diplomacy. The request of General Chehab for a deployment of American forces by sea to the port area; the appeal of President Chamoun "for Marines with tanks, quickly"; and the near-miss when the Lebanese tanks and artillery almost opened fire on the advancing Marine column; all these crises were dealt with successfully by the American diplomatic arm ashore.

(3) Once CINCSPECOME had arrived and established his command, there was a smooth and sure interplay of the military and diplomatic function in the carrying out of an exercise in limited war. Political advice impinged upon military decisions, and military decisions were taken with political as well as military ends in view. As indicated previously, the entire American establishment in Lebanon, diplomatic, military, and — here a word of well-earned praise — the private civilian community, worked together as a band of brothers.

In retrospect the American landing in Lebanon was a case history in the use of limited war and the practice of applied diplomacy. There can be no effective diplomacy without the existence of some form of power, whether military, economic or psychological. The use of military power in diplomacy can be either positive or negative. In the landing in Lebanon both elements of such power were present; but from the purely political point of view, the negative use of American military strength was the most effective at the time and the most lasting in long-range significance. This exercise in diplomatic and military cooperation was an historic illustration of the fact that diplomacy is the expression of national strength in terms of gentlemanly discourse.

CHAPTER VIII

The Chinese Attack on the
Himalayan Frontier of India, 1962

WE COME NOW to a limited war in Asia fought for the simple retention of strategic territory. This was the attack by Communist China against India on the Himalayan Frontier.

It will be recalled from the chapter on the war in Korea that Communist China struck twice in 1950, once into the Korean Peninsula against the power of the Free World represented by the United States and the United Nations and, in another direction and on interior lines, into the ancient theocracy of Tibet. On January 1, 1950, Mao Tse-tung proclaimed the "liberation of three million Tibetans from imperialist aggression" as a basic aim of the People's Liberation Army of China. In October 1950 his troops entered Tibet. In May 1951 Tibetan representatives came to Peking and signed a seventeen-point agreement which provided for Chinese occupation of Tibet but guaranteed the preservation of Buddhist institutions, the autonomy of the Tibetan government, and the status of the Dalai Lama (who repudiated this agreement when he escaped in 1959 from Tibet to India).[1]

1.

On April 29, 1954, the Ambassador of India in Peking signed with the Deputy Foreign Minister of China an agreement between the Republic of India and the People's Republic of China on trade and intercourse between the Tibet region of China and India. By this treaty India recognized

Chinese suzerainty over Tibet. By an irony of history, the preamble of the treaty enshrined the famous five principles of Panch Shila or peaceful coexistence which had first been introduced for the beguilement of Indians by Chou En-lai on December 31, 1953, at a reception for the Indian delegation which had arrived in Peking to negotiate the treaty on Tibet. These were the same principles of "mutual respect for each other's territorial integrity and sovereignty, mutual non-aggression, mutual non-interference in each other's internal affairs, equality and mutual benefit, and peaceful coexistence" [2] which in the following year became the leitmotif of the Bandung Conference and which for a number of years served as an opiate to dull the sensibilities of Nehru and Krishna Menon as to the true nature of Chinese Communism. Thus the Sino-Indian Treaty of 1954 accomplished two objectives for Mao Tse-tung: the recognition of Chinese dominion over a previously independent Himalayan State, and a soporific in the five principles of Panch Shila which would put Indian leaders safely to sleep until almost past the time of their awakening.

2.

China, having taken Tibet, found itself under the necessity of improving its military line of communications to that remote Himalayan plateau. Although Tibet is accessible through mountain passes from Szechuan to the west, the most feasible route is based on the principle that "the longest way round is the shortest way home." North of Tibet lies Sinkiang which is divided into two parts by the Tien Shan or Heavenly Mountains. To the north of this range lies the Djungaria Basin and to the south the Tarim Basin, called by the Chinese the Han-hai, or Dry Sea, extending 900 miles from east to west and 350 miles from north to south. This is the vast desert crossed by the Buddhist pilgrim, Hsuan

Tsang, in the seventh century on his way to India, and by Marco Polo in the thirteenth century. The Chinese Communists built at immense labor a road around the rim of this forbidding desert, linking the strategic Cherchen-Yarkand road with a southward extension to Gartok which comes near the border of Kashmir and crosses that part of Ladakh which is called the Aksai Chin, "the Desert of White Stones." Between 1955 and 1958 the Chinese completed a motor road across this finger of Ladakh, unknown to the slumbering Indians whose territory it was claimed to be. The road starts from Yehcheng in Sinkiang and runs as far as Gartok in Tibet for a length of 666 miles, in which 100 miles run through the contested territory of the Aksai Chin.

The frontier of India with China in the west abuts on Sinkiang. There is then a zone of Himalayan buffer states running across the north of India — Nepal, Sikkim, and Bhutan — before once more there is a contiguous frontier between India and Tibet in the North East Frontier Agency or NEFA. Here the boundary since 1914 has been the so-called McMahon Line, named after the British chief delegate* who signed the definitive map on April 27, 1914, during the Simla Conference between the representatives of the governments of India, China and Tibet. The McMahon Line definitively traced the boundaries of that Himalayan buffer state, kept intact on the Roof of the World by the imperial rivalries of Britain, Russia and China. Successive Chinese governments refused to acknowledge the authenticity of the McMahon Line, despite the fact that the plenipotentiary of the government at Peking had signed the map.[4]

Once the Indians had discovered the existence of the Chi-

---

* Sir Henry McMahon years later, in an address to the Royal Society of Arts in 1935, made a sound distinction between a "frontier" and a "boundary." The former meant "a wide tract of border land which, perhaps by virtue of its ruggedness or other difficulty, served as a buffer between two states." A boundary on the other hand was a clearly defined line, "delimited" or "demarcated." [3]

nese military road across Ladakh there were border skirmishes between patrols with casualties on both sides; and, on
August 31, 1958, Nehru gave the Indian Parliament details of
the Chinese incursions into Ladakh which he described as "a
barren and uninhabited region, 17,000 feet high and without
a vestige of grass."

3.

The Sino-Indian border dispute dragged on for four years
and resulted in the publication by the government of India
of a monumental White Paper[5] consisting of ten volumes of
diplomatic correspondence, statements and maps. In addition there was an equally monumental Officials' Report[6] in
which Indian and Chinese experts set forth their contesting
claims. Beyond any doubt the Indian research was the better documented and more faithful to the realities, not only of
the historical and traditional frontiers, but also of the un-
doubted fact that as a rule both in the west and in the eastern sector the watershed, or the highest range of mountains,
formed the boundary between India and Tibet, India and
Sinkiang.

Without going into detail over this mountainous correspondence, Himalayan in its proportions, it is accurate to
say that the Chinese with little regard for geographical or
historical evidence played their game to keep what they had
already taken in the Aksai Chin and to play off this de facto
possession of territory by making other claims to the east
along the so-called "illegal McMahon Line." They steadfastly and for propaganda purposes pretended to regard the
McMahon boundary as illegitimate because of its "imperialist
origin" and because it had never been recognized by any Chinese government. In effect, therefore, as Nehru succinctly
put it, the Chinese were seeking to wield a "Chinese brush
painted over large chunks of another's territory."[7]

While continuing to press Nehru to grant concessions in
Ladakh in return for Chinese readiness to withdraw their
claims south of the McMahon Line in the North East Frontier
Agency, the Chinese likewise sought to bring external pressure on India by signing other border settlement agreements
with India's neighbors. Thus in January 1961 they reached
an agreement with Burma on the Sino-Burmese border and
two months later signed a border agreement with Nepal in
March 1961. What really alarmed the Indians however was
the announcement early in 1961 of a desire to undertake
border talks with the government of Pakistan. This touched
Nehru on his rawest nerve since Sino-Pakistani conversations
would involve the frontier of Kashmir which the Indian Government proclaimed to be wholly Indian. In early May 1962,
Peking announced a Sino-Pakistan agreement to "locate and
align their common border" and a year later, on March 2,
1963, Pakistan and China signed a boundary agreement.* [8]
It was therefore not surprising that the Indian Government
rejected a Chinese proposal to negotiate a new agreement to
replace the treaty of April 29, 1954, which was due to expire
on June 3, 1962 — the treaty whose preamble so persuasively
proclaimed the five principles of "peaceful co-existence." [9]

4.

India now embarked on a highly risky policy. Although it
lacked the economic power base to stand up to Red China
and was markedly inferior in military strength, the Indian
High Command, backed by press and public opinion, pushed
Nehru and the reluctant Defense Minister, Khrishna Menon,

* What will more disturb the government of India will be the disclosure
in 1966 that Pakistan is building a strategic road through its part of Kashmir,
up the valleys of the Indus and Hunza rivers to the Khunjerab Pass, whence
the road connects with the highway system of Chinese Sinkiang.

into a series of "nibbling" military operations in Ladakh, threatening the Chinese road across the Aksai Chin. Nehru himself said early in 1961 that India had built six military posts in the Ladakh area behind which there was a logistical organization based on a network of new mountain roads. "We shall continue to build up these things," he said, "so that ultimately we may be in a position to take effective action to recover such territory as is in the possession of the Chinese. We do not want a war, but whatever steps we take we must be strong enough to pursue them to a logical conclusion." [10]

The Chinese now commenced a series of increasingly clear warnings that India was in for trouble if it should persist in its policy of "nibbling" into the Aksai Chin. Again the Chinese linked the eastern frontier along the so-called "illegal McMahon Line" to provide an eventual *quid pro quo* against their main objective, the strategic highway across "the Desert of White Stones." Thus on November 2, 1961, the Chinese called upon India to "speedily change" its "very erroneous and dangerous" strategy.[11] In the same month they warned that if India continued to disturb the status quo on the western frontier "The Chinese Government would have every reason to send troops to cross the so-called 'McMahon Line' and enter the vast area between the crest of the Himalayas and their southern foot." [12] Surely there could have been no clearer warning than that. The government of India replied that if the Chinese did cross the McMahon Line it would be considered as a further act of aggression which would be resisted.

It is necessary now to undertake an essay in psychoanalysis of Chinese Communist political mentality. Red China in 1961 and 1962 was taken by a psychosis of fear that the United States, the arch villain of the "imperialists," was orchestrating a gigantic pincers movement with the ready acquiescence if not connivance of Khrushchev and the U.S.S.R. To the analysts in Peking, relying upon the dogma of Mao Tse-tung and such distorted information as they derived from their own news agency, Hsin Hua, there seemed to be building up a renewed threat of possible invasion by forces of the Nationalist Chinese based on Taiwan. In addition there had been an unarmed uprising in Sinkiang where thousands of Kazaks had revolted against the Chinese regime and fled to sanctuary in the U.S.S.R. This was the so-called "Sinkiang Exodus." To complete the circle of imagined threat, now Nehru, the former apostle of non-alignment and the practitioner of the principles of Panch Shila, was proving unexpectedly tough in the Aksai Chin.

The Chinese Communist leaders built up a curious hate-love complex over Nehru. He was at one and the same time a potential ally and a foremost spokesman for Peking, but always in the back of their minds lingered the doubt how such a bourgeois could sincerely practice the principles which he professed. Furthermore the puzzled policymakers in Peking could not understand why it was that Nehru could not more absolutely impose his will upon the people and press of India. Focusing on Nehru through their own Chinese Communist binoculars, they did not comprehend that he was subservient to pressures of nationalism the same as lesser mortals. Furthermore there was always at the back of their minds the increasing doubt that Nehru, true to his bourgeois background, might ultimately become the willing tool of the "Western imperialists." Thus the Chinese leaders began to view Nehru as a "two-faced" neutral who in fact might work against the strategic interests of China. Therefore the contradictory Chinese attitude toward Nehru went through a pendulum motion between the desire to "unite" with the leader of India and simultaneously to "struggle" against him.

5.

The Chinese warnings of impending action became more explicit. In a note of August 27, 1962, the government at Peking stated, "if the Indian side should overdo it, the Chinese side will have resort to self-defense, and the Indian side must bear the responsibility for all the consequences arising therefrom." [13]

New Delhi replied that it would not enter into discussions "under duress or continuing threat of force"; and on October 12 Nehru instructed the Indian Army "to free Indian territory in the North East Frontier Agency of Chinese intruders." [14] On October 14 the *People's Daily* of Peking asked Nehru "to pull back from the brink of the precipice." [15] On October 20 both sides reached the brink.

On that day Chinese infantry stormed over the Thagla Ridge in the North East Frontier Agency sector and overran an Indian brigade of 5000 men positioned along the Kachilang River. By the 24th of October the invading Chinese had occupied the entire region of Towang. A month later by November 21 they had occupied the Se-la, Bomdi-la and Chakoo sectors. The strategic threat of the invasion was clear. The Chinese Communists were striking for the Siliguri Corridor between Nepal and East Pakistan. Once through this narrow aperture they could fan out into the plains of Assam and before them envision the whole of the Brahmaputra Valley and East Bengal with their rich plantations of jute and tea, the fertile fields of Assam, and the oil resources of that region.* [16]

---

* The Chinese early in this century had threatened Assam from Tibet. In 1910 the Chinese Resident, Chao Erh-teng, had occupied Lhasa and forced the Dalai Lama to flee to India, as did his young successor in 1959. Chao Erh-teng required "the monkey people," as he called the Assam tribesmen, to tender their submission. So alarmed were the British that Sir Michael

On October 29 Indian defense officials requested United States military assistance. The U.S. rushed in sixty planes loaded with five million dollars worth of automatic weapons, heavy mortars, and land mines. Twelve C-130 transport aircraft with U.S. crews and maintenance teams arrived in New Delhi to fly Indian troops and equipment to the battle zone. The United Kingdom, Canada and Australia were quick to supply additional aid to India.[18]

The Chinese Dragon paused on the high crest of the Himalayas but its claws did not stretch out to the plains of Assam. The Chinese Tibetan Army had a supply line 5000 miles long and before it in the lowlands was a regrouped and restrengthened Indian army. Furthermore the limited objective of a truly limited war had already been achieved. By making a feint on the left flank into the North East Frontier Agency China retained its hold on the strategic goal of the entire exercise — the vital highway across the Aksai Chin. Furthermore, India now knew that when China said it would strike it could strike, and that there was truth in Mao Tse-tung's dictum that "our strategy is to pit one against ten, while our tactic is to pit ten against one."

In the Himalayan fighting the Chinese People's Army was markedly superior to its Indian opposition, although the numbers were not so unevenly matched as might have been supposed. There were somewhat over 100,000 Chinese Communist troops in the Tibetan military region. These were organized into three infantry divisions, nine independent in-

---

Hirtzel of the Political and Secret Department at the India Office wrote on January 12, 1911: "if anything goes wrong in Assam, there would be a very voiceful opinion against us. . . . Think of the howl the planters would let out, and the rise in the price of tea!"

And G. A. Neville, from 1913 Political Officer for the Western Sector of the Assam Hills, warned in 1928 that "there is no doubt that as soon as China settles down this Tibetan frontier will become of great importance. China still has its eyes on Tibet, and . . . should China gain control of Tibet, the Towang country is particularly adapted for a secret and easy entrance into India." [17]

fantry regiments and artillery regiments, one cavalry regiment, and five border defense regiments.

For the thrust on two fronts, however, the Chinese deployed in Ladakh 7000 troops against an equal number of Indian troops: on the Chinese side one infantry regiment, one cavalry regiment and border defense elements against elements of one Indian brigade. In addition the Indians had one division in reserve in Ladakh. The Chinese uniformly drove the Indians out of that portion of Ladakh to which they laid claim. In the North East Frontier Agency the Chinese offensive was launched with six infantry regiments and the defeat of the solitary Indian infantry brigade in the Towang area was accomplished by three infantry regiments with supporting artillery. Here also the Indians had one infantry division deployed in a defensive posture on the Se-La Pass. In the North East Frontier Agency area the Indian army numbered 35,000 troops with 15,000 committed to forward area defense against 20,000 Chinese.

However, if the numbers were roughly equal, the Chinese were superior primarily by reason of acclimatization to the high Tibetan plateau and to better lines of communication. They also, as in Korea, had perfected techniques of attacks at night and were unhampered by heavy equipment. The Indian GI, or Jawan, was burdened by an unnecessary kit weighing seventy pounds and was totally unaccustomed to fighting at 17,000 feet. In addition, the Indian lines of communication, although shorter than the Chinese, were made impassable by the monsoon rains and by the abrupt terrain, whereas the Chinese were attacking downhill from the Tibetan plateau.

6.

On November 21 the government at Peking announced a cease-fire along the entire Sino-Indian frontier from midnight

November 21. Beginning December 1, Chinese frontier guards would withdraw to positions twenty kilometers behind the line of "actual control" which existed between China and India on November 7, 1959.[19] To this Nehru replied in a letter to Chou En-lai dated January 1, 1963:

> It would be obvious to any one who looks at the position objectively that this scale of military clashes and such large scale advance into Indian territory could not have occurred unless there was a pre-planned and carefully concerted aggressive move by the Chinese forces. Under the Chinese declaration of unilateral cease-fire and withdrawals, the Chinese forces propose to withdraw from the bulk of this area, but they stipulate a specific condition that the limited defensive measures against Chinese aggression taken by India both in the Eastern and Western sectors should not be restored. All sorts of fallacious arguments regarding the line of actual control as on November 7, 1959, the need for disengagement of forces etc are advanced to enable the Chinese side to retain its gains of the latest aggression since 8 September 1962, in the Western and Eastern sector. No amount of wordy argument can hide this position of advantage that the Chinese Government seek to retain as the spoils of their latest aggression.[20]

On December 10–12, 1962, the six so-called Afro-Asian nonaligned countries* met at Colombo on the invitation of Mrs. Bandaranaike, the Prime Minister of Ceylon. This conference proposed that the existing *de facto* cease-fire continue; that the Chinese carry out their twenty kilometer withdrawal as proposed in the letters of Chou En-lai to Nehru of November 21 and November 28; and that the Indian Government should keep its existing military positions.[21] Nehru wrote Prime Minister Bandaranaike on January 26 that, after receiving clarification from the Colombo powers on January

* Burma, Cambodia, Ceylon, Ghana, Indonesia and the United Arab Republic.

13, the government of India was prepared to accept the Colombo proposals *in toto*.[22]

Almost a year later the government in Peking, while professing readiness to undertake negotiations in principle on the basis of the Colombo proposals, and concluding its note with the stylized phrase, "the Ministry of Foreign Affairs avails itself of this opportunity to renew to the Indian Embassy the assurances of its highest consideration," could not refrain from resorting to Communist dialectic:

> The Indian Government does not have the least desire to hold negotiations with China, but has every determination to wage long-term cold war against China. It is known to all that the Indian Government has been begging for large amounts of military assistance from U.S. imperialism for arms expansion and war preparation, and has recently even openly colluded with the United States and Britain in preparing to conduct joint air manoeuvres.[23]

7.

The Chinese attack on the Himalayan frontier of India was a limited war in the classical sense of limitation both of objectives and theater of conflict. However, as in the cases of Greece and Korea, this intended limited war on the Communist side broadened to unlimited consequences: it pushed India from the delusions of Panch Shila and nonalignment onto the borders of the Free World.

The Chinese objective was strategic and unequivocal. In 1950 Mao Tse-tung had three military operations in prospect, two of his own choosing and one thrust upon him. The first was to attack the forces of Nationalist China on Taiwan. This was frustrated by Stalin's exercise in limited war in Korea and President Truman's immediate response with the Seventh Fleet. The second was to invade Tibet, which was liberally advertised in advance and efficiently carried out by the Third People's Army. The third, which was forced upon Mao by force of events and circumstance, was his engagement with the Fourth People's Army in war against the United States in Korea.

Tibet having been occupied and returned once more as an "autonomous region" of China, it was essential from the strategic point of view to maintain the new line of communications around the deserts of Sinkiang from Peking and Central China to Lhasa. To this effect the strategic road was built across that part of Ladakh called the Aksai Chin to Gartok with its main east-west extension running for hundreds of miles to Nagchhukha and thence south to Lhasa. It was the Indian threat to this segment of the jugular vein to Tibet which caused the Chinese reaction in limited war. Although the main military thrust was in NEFA, the North East Frontier Agency, this was at all times a strategical feint: the accent was on the strategic frontier at Ladakh.*

The Chinese coolly assessed the situation and calculated that if force had to be used they would be fighting the Indians alone and that they had preponderant strength to win their objectives. Having won that objective they unilaterally declared a cease-fire and withdrew their forces. However, important dividends were earned by this exercise in limited war. The Chinese Communists indicated clearly to other Asians that the Red Dragon had claws. The humiliating defeat of the ill-prepared Indian Army showed Asia's second

---

* As a matter of fact, the British proposed in a Note dated March 14, 1899, from Sir Claude MacDonald, H. B. M.'s Minister in Peking, to the Tsungli Yamen, that the frontier between British India and Sinkiang in Ladakh divide the Aksai Chin on a line which would have left the present Sinkiang-Tibet road on the Chinese side. To this Note the Chinese Government made no reply.[24] It is interesting that the British official who first suggested this boundary line, George Macartney, British representative in Kashgar from 1890 to 1918, was half-Chinese, and his father was advisor to the Imperial Chinese Legation in London.

most populous nation who was the most important indigenous military power in Asia — mainland China. On the philosophy that "the enemy of my enemy is my friend," Peking seduced Pakistan into an uneasy relationship of temporary friendship. This was to have important consequences in eroding the cement uniting the already shaky structures of SEATO and CENTO — but the story here is not ended.

On the Indian side abundant mistakes were made. In the first place, under the opiate influence of Panch Shila, Nehru and Krishna Menon for years forbade themselves to suspect that Peking could be less than perfect. This is shown by the astounding ignorance of the Indian Government of the fact that the strategic road across the Desert of White Stones, the Aksai Chin, was being built by some 3000 Chinese and Tibetan coolies over a two-year period.

The second mistake was military. The Indian General Staff deluded Nehru into the assumption that their policy of "nibbling" at Ladakh, outflanking Chinese frontier outposts, could successfully be carried out without a sufficient power base to sustain the operation. Faced with extraordinary difficulties of environment, including the necessity to patrol and fight at an altitude three miles above sea level and with precarious lines of supply, the Indian Army was clearly not ready for the Chinese riposte which followed on October 20, 1962.

Furthermore, the Indians refused to heed repeated Chinese warnings. Had they read the experience of the Americans in Korea when the warning came loud and clear (but was discounted) through their own Indian Ambassador in Peking, they should have known that there comes a time in the councils of the Communist Government of China when communication is explicit and consequences follow.

And finally Nehru, dedicated to the five principles of peaceful coexistence, found himself, although the strongest man in India, pushed by the effervescence of nationalism, by the power of the press and an eloquent opposition, into making a stand which he himself believed in but did not dare at the outset to become adamant upon.

8.

In terms of world strategy it is an interesting coincidence that the two giant Communist powers confronted free nations simultaneously in October 1962. Russia was, in Khrushchev's personality, "eyeball to eyeball" with President Kennedy over the placement of strategic rockets in Cuba, and Mao Tse-tung at a greater reprieve of distance confronted Nehru across the crest of the Himalayas. However, there was no connection between the Cuban crisis and Peking's decision to fight a limited war with India. This was not a repetition of the Korean War, where Stalin's attack by proxy troops had to be sustained by Mao Tse-tung when the proxy troops were defeated. The Sino-Indian episode in limited war had no real relevance to the Cuban exercise as a limited aspect of general war. In fact, by the summer of 1962 the mutual antagonism between Moscow and Peking was so intense that the possibility of mutual support was excluded. When Khrushchev in the middle of October sought the support of Peking for his Cuban missile adventure, the Chinese out of hand rejected his approach and implicitly criticized him as a possible silent partner of the Indians.

In assessment of global strategy Peking made a mistake. It won its limited war for retention of a strategic road to one of the most inaccessible areas of Asia, Tibet, once more a makeweight in the balance of power. But to reinsure its title to Tibet, Peking lost the friendship of India.

This is a fact of monumental importance. It likewise goes

to prove that not always are the Communists as smart as they pretend to be or as their frightened opponents claim they are. Mao Tse-tung by no means in this exchange came out the strategic victor.

Thus the limited war fought by Communist China for possession of the remote and airless Askai Chin, for the road which circumnavigates the Han-hai, or Dry Sea, had almost unlimited consequences. It pushed India into more effective self-defense and put up a potential barrier to Chinese Communist expansion.* The channels for this Chinese Communist expansion were narrowed, the pressure intensified, made more explosive. In shifting from the Han-hai, or Dry Sea, to the Nan-hai or South China Sea, the purpose again was dominance. This time, dominance of the Straits which link the Pacific and Indian Oceans. The objectives geographically were Malaysia and Indonesia; the route lay through Laos, Cambodia, and Viet Nam. Once again the land power of China would meet the sea power of the United States. But first there was France.

* Professor Owen Lattimore, who is not widely regarded by certain elements of the U.S. Senate as being anti-Communist Chinese, wrote in a book in 1928 that the Chinese are "not passive, but thoroughly imbued with the instinct and spirit of domination, an expansionist people whose expansion has been temporarily checked by their inability to cope with better armed expansionists . . . Wherever the Chinese have secured (if only for a few days) some measure of power and initiative, they have made it clear . . . in spite of the conflictions of domestic politics, that to their minds one of the chief functions of Chinese power is to assert Chinese domination — domination, not equality — over every race that comes within the scope of Chinese action." [25]

CHAPTER IX

"Wars of National Liberation": The French Colonial War in Viet Nam, 1946–1950

The big dilemma is, you can't win the people until you defeat the military forces, and you can't defeat the military forces until you win the people.[*]

But first there was France.

In this study of limited war the conflict in Indochina is the first in which we address ourselves to a colonial limited war; and the first in which we study the latter-day phenomenon of the Communist political invention of "wars of national liberation."

1.

The origins of the Indochinese struggle for independence go back a long way — almost a century. In this study we shall be concerned less with the struggle for independence of Cambodia, which was achieved with relative ease under the dynamic leadership of a supposedly puppet king of the French, Prince Norodom Sihanouk, who turned out to be far from a puppet; and the attainment of an unsought and precarious "independence" in the Kingdom of Laos, a country which the author once described in an official report to the Secretary of State as "a long land inhabited by Lotus

[*] Letter to the author from Colonel Leo Dulacki, USMC, Headquarters, Third Marine Amphibious Force, Da Nang, December 23, 1965.

Eaters." Rather, our concern will be with the struggle for independence in Viet Nam, which began as a simple colonial war of definitely limited proportions and evolved into a full-grown Communist-style "war of national liberation."

It has been said that colonialism, by aggravating social tensions, nurtures the forces which are destined ultimately to destroy it.[1] Certainly the operation of the French empire in the Far East became increasingly an anachronism, and the effort of those political, colonial and military leaders who strove mightily to put the clock back resulted inevitably in their defeat. The fact that the colonial war in Viet Nam later broadened out into a Communist-style "war of national liberation" must not blind the student of history to the original character of the conflict and the subtle political sea-change which came over the struggle in the course of a decade's fighting.

In its eighty years of colonial control France administered the three ancient Vietnamese kingdoms of Tonkin, Annam, and Cochin-China as an economic entity and to the benefit of the metropolitan power. In Viet Nam there was considerable economic sense in this arrangement because the surplus rice of the Mekong delta in the south was sent to feed the superabundant population of Tonkin in the north, where in turn the rich anthracite coal mines of Honghai and such industry as existed in Viet Nam could supply the fertile southern region of Cochin-China. In between, in Annam, except for the ancient imperial capital of Hué by its malodorous River of Perfumes and a few coastal towns such as Nhatrang and Tourane (now the U.S. Marine Base at Danang) the central highlands of this area were sparsely populated. In fact in the mountains themselves — in the beautiful blue-gray pine forests of the *Chaine Annamite* — there were few Vietnamese at all. Here lived the Montagnards, derisively called Moi or savages by the Vietnamese:

aboriginal hill people living in stilt-legged thatched huts, in communal long houses, who had little relationship with the Confucian culture of the rest of Viet Nam.

Taking Viet Nam as a whole, French policy can only be described as one of neo-mercantilism. The colonies were expected to supply raw materials and provide markets for the manufactured products of the mother country. The interests of the colony were always subservient to those of France.

This policy was implemented by a variety of means. For one, there was effective financial control of capital investment. This was exercised through the ubiquitous Banque de l'Indochine, ostensibly a private institution but policy-wise an arm of the French Government. So effective were the controls on capital investment, both through the Banque de l'Indochine and government regulation, that in 1938 95 per cent of foreign capital invested in Viet Nam was French.[2] Vietnamese businessmen were forced to pay higher taxes than their French counterparts. Foreign trade was restricted entirely to French firms. In addition, the alcohol and opium monopolies were official and in various provinces quotas were fixed for the forced consumption of these two socially suspect commodities.[3] The Vietnamese peasant tilling his tenant's land in a rice paddy saw perhaps little difference between the rule of the mandarins of Annam and Cochin-China and the later rule of the French colonial landlord, although he may have changed the scene of his labors to the great rubber plantations. However, to the newly risen middle class it was galling to find that the economy of the country was in the hands of the colonial power, scarcely mitigated by the entrepreneurial Chinese merchants of Cholon. From this point of view it was easy to make the transition to regarding the colonial power as "an imperialistic exploiter."

With the advent of World War II the Japanese replaced the French as exploiters; but at least these new masters were

Orientals. The Vietnamese noted with appreciation the fact that the once proud white power — France — had not only been defeated by a new barbarian named Hitler in Europe, but, before their eyes, had been humbled by Asiatic empire. The author remembers an anecdote told in Saigon relating to the days of the Japanese occupation. There was a certain Japanese colonel who every morning took his breakfast in one of the French sidewalk cafés on Rue Catinat. Each morning he had the same repast. He would order fried eggs, sunny-side up, and then, ostentatiously before a crowd of appreciative Vietnamese, would separate the whites from the yellows.

The Japanese occupation of Indochina served as a catalyst to the movement for independence. The Vichy-appointed Governor General of Indochina, Vice Admiral Jean Decoux, who played a lengthy and skillful game to maintain the French administration intact, despite its Japanese military overlordship, sought to gain favor with the Vietnamese by liberalizing the government and bringing more Vietnamese into the colonial regime. However, in widening access to office for the Vietnamese he provided the future revolutionary movement with a cadre of trained and experienced officials. Even Decoux's national youth movement for sports, organized on a paramilitary basis, later turned out to be a hotbed of Vietnamese nationalism.[4]

When the Japanese finally intervened in force on March 9, 1945, imprisoning Admiral Decoux and taking over outright the governance of Viet Nam, they turned over most of the administration to Vietnamese officials with Japanese advisers. Furthermore, in liberating between 8000 and 10,000 political prisoners they opened the Pandora's box of Poulo Condor, the French Asiatic equivalent of Devil's Island.

Another factor contributing to the outbreak of a colonial limited war in Viet Nam was the increasing sense of frustration of the Vietnamese intellectuals. They were educated, some of them in France or in French lycées in Saigon, in the great traditions of French freedom: of *Liberté, Égalité, Fraternité*. Yet under the rigid French colonial system there was neither liberty, equality nor fraternity in Viet Nam as between the colonial presence and the indigenous population. David Schoenbrun, the CBS correspondent, quotes Ho Chi Minh as saying, "It was not in Moscow that I learned what revolution was, but in Paris, in the capital of Liberty, Equality, and Fraternity." [5]

While many of the intellectuals discontented themselves with grumbling over their tea cups in Saigon and swelling the ranks of the so-called *Attentistes* or fence sitters, there were others, intensely nationalistic but non-Communist, who worked openly or secretly to bring about the eventual day of independence from colonial rule. Such a leader was Pham Huy Quat, a young doctor from the Tonkin, who became a leader of the Dai Viet Party. It was Quat, later a Minister of Defense and recently Prime Minister (1965), whose family the author evacuated by air from Hanoi after the partition of Viet Nam in 1954.

2.

However, there were other intellectual leaders who eventually were to form the nucleus of the Communist insurrection against French rule, under the name of Viet Minh. Everyone has heard of the legendary Ho Chi Minh and of the military victor of Dien Bien Phu, General Vo Nguyen Giap, presently Minister of Defense in Hanoi. The name of Pham Van Dong, the present Prime Minister of the People's Democratic Republic of Viet Nam, is also known. Less familiar to Western readers is Truong Chinh (his real name is Dan Xuan Khu), a principal member of the Lao Dong

Party and its principal theoretician. But always we return to Ho Chi Minh.

The name of Ho Chi Minh is so much tied to current history that his links with the past seem almost an anachronism. In 1913–1914 a pastry cook under the great chef, Escoffier, at the Carlton Hotel in London, later in Paris in 1917 he knew the French Socialists, including Leon Blum, Marcel Cachin, and Charles Longuet, the nephew of Karl Marx. In a rented blue suit, Nguyen Ai Quoc,* as he was then known by a *nom de plume* (Nguyen, the Patriot), Ho Chi Minh sat in the Versailles anteroom of Woodrow Wilson and Lloyd George, hoping to present his modest eight-point program for "internal autonomy; liberty of association, press and movement; amnesty for political prisoners; equality of rights between French and Vietnamese; abolition of 'forced consumption of alcohol and opium,' forced labor and the gabelle." [7]

This list of aspirations of the leader of Vietnamese nationalism is cited for its diffidence of scope. Had Ho Chi Minh's program been accepted in 1919 by the inventor of "self-determination," perhaps this chapter would not have been written. Likewise there is cited the reaction of the leaders at Versailles: a cold shoulder — "*on lui fait faire antichambre.*"

Since the objectives of limited war are political, it is necessary to study the personalities of the politicians who formulate these objectives and carry the war to victory or defeat. Even the undertaker of the Centurions, General of the Army Paul Ely, conceded that the Viet Minh "were waging a revolutionary war whose political aspects were essentially inseparable from its military aspects." [8] Therefore in studying the colonial war in Indochina which led to the "war of

---

* Ho Chi Minh has had many names. He was most probably born Nguyen Van Thanh.[6]

national liberation" in Viet Nam, the life of Ho Chi Minh is in effect a history of the revolutionary movement.

Following his rebuff at the Versailles peace conference, Ho Chi Minh went to Russia in 1924 and was a student at the University of the Workers of the Orient in Moscow. 1925 or 1926 found him as a translator and interpreter for the Komintern agent, Borodin, in Canton. Here the future Ho Chi Minh undoubtedly met Mao Tse-tung and Chiang Kai-shek. He founded a revolutionary journal, Thanh-Nien (Youth) and established the so-called League of the Oppressed Peoples of Asia. It was at this time, in 1926, that a Vietnamese student at the Chinese Military Academy at Whampoa, one Pham Van Dong, met Nguyen Ai Quoc, the future Ho Chi Minh. Pham Van Dong was the son of the Chef de Cabinet of the Emperor Duy Tan[9] and because of his aristocratic lineage can rightly be styled the Marxist Mandarin. It is he who at the present time is Prime Minister of the Communist government in North Viet Nam.

The next years saw Ho Chi Minh constantly on the move. When in 1927 Chiang Kai-shek turned against the Communists, Ho, then in Shanghai, fled toward Russia, reaching Berlin in 1927. In the next year he turned up in Thailand disguised as a Buddhist monk, proselytizing among the Vietnamese *Colons*. He walked on foot across part of Burma back to South China via Yunnan, reaching Kwei-lin, the capital of Kwangsi Province, at the end of December 1929. On January 6, 1930, Ho Chi Minh founded the Indochinese Communist Party, the Dong-Duong Cong-San Dan.[10]

In Viet Nam itself, particularly in Tonkin and in Northern Annam, the Nationalists were growing restive against French rule. On February 9, 1930, Vietnamese troops of the Yen-Bay garrison mutinied and murdered their officers. This revolt was put down with firmness by the French. Later in the year, on September 12, 1930, six thousand desperate and starving peasants formed the "Xo-Viet Nghe-An" and marched toward the provincial capital of Vinh. This uprising was put down with great severity by the French military. Ho Chi Minh succeeded in fleeing to Hong Kong, but Pham Van Dong, Ton Duc Thang and Vo Nguyen Giap were imprisoned on Poulo Condor.[11] The French had identified their enemies and thought that by stern police action they had scotched the snake of Asian nationalism.

Ho Chi Minh was arrested on his arrival in Hong Kong but released, thanks to the efforts of an effective British barrister. He then tried to sail secretly to England but was discovered at Singapore and returned to Hong Kong. Thence he escaped to Amoy and apparently at this time married a Chinese. After 1933, however, the record is blank. For eight years there was no word of Nguyen Ai Quoc. The French Sûreté declared him dead.[12] But Nguyen Ai Quoc turned up once more at Kwei-lin in 1941 and was imprisoned by the Chinese authorities. For eighteen months he languished in the *Kang*, the Chinese equivalent of the stocks. However, in 1943 the war lord of Kwangsi Province, General Chang Fa-kwei, released him. The Vietnamese nationalist leader named Nguyen Ai Quoc who had entered prison eighteen months before emerged as the Vietnamese nationalist leader, Ho Chi Minh — "He Who Illuminates." A more practical consideration was the fact that since Chang Fa-kwei had failed to inform Chiang Kai-shek of his captive's presence, by changing his name Nguyen Ai Quoc escaped the notice of the Political Police.[13]

The reason the war lord of Kwangsi Province released Ho Chi Minh was that he wished to use the Vietnamese nationalist movement against both the Japanese and French. It is important to note that, despite his education with the Komintern in Moscow, Ho Chi Minh at this period did not identify himself as a Communist but as a simon pure Vietnamese nationalist. In fact the eighth session of the Indo-chinese Communist Party's Central Committee which met in South China in 1941 identified the central task as "the formation of an alliance with all social classes and political parties, patriotic and revolutionary groups, religious groups and all people fighting the Japanese and desiring national independence from France and Japan." It was at this time that a new united front organization was created called the Viet-Nam Doc-Lap Dong Minh (League for Independence of Viet Nam), better known by the short form: Viet Minh.[14]

3.

The newly baptized Ho Chi Minh, The Illuminator, was shortly invited to spread his light with the OSS in China. He went to Kunming in February 1945 to meet the OSS Chief, Colonel Paul Helliwell. According to this officer the OSS refused to give Ho Chi Minh arms against the Japanese unless he promised not to use them against the French. However, later it seems clear that the OSS did parachute some small quantities of arms and ammunition to the Viet Minh insurgents.[15] In August 1945, Ho Chi Minh wrote to an OSS acquaintance asking him to pass a message to the United States Government to support independence for Viet Nam at the recently created United Nations. Ho concluded his letter with these prophetic words, "If the U.N. should forget its solemn promise [to grant independence to colonial peoples] and if it does not give independence to Indochina, we shall continue to fight until we get it." [16]

The moment of truth was now rapidly approaching. With the defeat of the Japanese and the abdication of the puppet "Emperor" Bao Dai, there was an administrative vacuum in North Viet Nam and the Viet Minh were quick to establish a government in Hanoi in August 1945. They operated from a secure political base since the Viet Minh had for some time organized villages in the Viet Bac district northeast of Hanoi near the Chinese frontier. The leadership realized that it was essential to perfect a firm political organization before undertaking the obligations of government or entering into the phase of guerrilla warfare. Following the precepts of General Giap, "armed insurrection was given a secondary role and was not to be undertaken until such time as political indoctrination was well advanced." [17]

Although the Viet Minh proclaimed the independence of the Democratic People's Republic of Viet Nam on September 2, 1945, in Hanoi, their claim to independence was short-lived. The Allied powers decreed otherwise. In the summer of 1945 the 16th parallel was agreed upon as the boundary between Lord Louis Mountbatten's Southeast Asia Command which was to occupy the lower half of Viet Nam, while China Theater, where General Wedemeyer was Chief of Operations, would occupy the North. This meant that the Tonkin, where the Viet Minh government had been established at Hanoi, was to be occupied by Chinese Nationalist troops. However, during late August even before the arrival of Allied units in Viet Nam a series of Franco-British agreements had recognized French sovereignty in Indochina.[18]

By January 1, 1946, in addition to British forces in South Viet Nam, the French had 30,000 troops and presently took over entirely from the British Command. In the North the Chinese Nationalist Army of Occupation under General Lu Han recognized the DRV Government as the existing regime, responsible only to General Lu Han for administration. In fact it seems probable that Lu Han's master, Generalissimo Chiang Kai-shek, secretly desired to see an independent Viet Nam.

However, Mao Tse-tung had occupied Manchuria and it became necessary for Chiang Kai-shek to withdraw his forces from Tonkin and redeploy them to this northern front. It was in these circumstances that on February 28, 1946, French and Chinese representatives signed an agreement providing for the withdrawal of all Chinese forces from Indochina by March 31, 1946, in return for major concessions by France.[19] The French were once more suzerain in all of Viet Nam. On March 6 they signed a preliminary convention with the Democratic Republic of Viet Nam at Hanoi, permitting French military units to return to the territory under the control of the DRV. In view of the eight-year war which later ensued the comment of the French historian Devilliers that France was "the first, before Holland, before England, even before America, to reach an agreement with Asiatic Nationalism" seems ironic.[20]

The agreement of March 6, 1946, between Ho Chi Minh and the representative of De Gaulle, Jean Sainteny, recognized Viet Nam "as a free state within the French Union with its own parliament, army, and finances," but left the decision on "the exact status of Viet Nam as a member of the Indochina Federation and the French Union . . . [and] the question of diplomatic representation" for a later conference. The future of Cochin-China was to be decided by referendum.[21]

The last attempt at a negotiated settlement between Ho Chi Minh and the French took place later in 1946 during the summer, at Fontainebleau. Ho Chi Minh, at least at this stage, was anxious to reach a political understanding with France and a political settlement. On September 14 he signed a *modus vivendi* covering the economic, financial, and cultural relations between France and Viet Nam and calling for a cease-fire between French troops and Vietnamese guerrillas by October 31. The agreement also provided for a resumption of talks in January of the following year.[22] However, Ho Chi Minh was not able to secure French

agreement to the idea of an independent Viet Nam within
the framework of the French Union. On September 16 as he
left Paris Ho exclaimed, perhaps in despair, "Do not let me
leave this way; arm me against those who seek to defeat me.
You will have no reason to regret it." [23] As the negotiator of
the agreement with the DRV, Jean Sainteny, was later to
write as the title of his book, it was *L'histoire d'une Paix
Manquée* — the story of a lost peace.

4.

A new pro-consul was sent out to Indochina in the person
of Admiral Thierry d'Argenlieu. In the metropole it seemed
perfectly just and understandable that France, which had
undergone such humiliating defeats, should reassert its sovereignty in Southeast Asia. Even the French Communists
under Thorez did not lift a voice in protest. However, it
will be recalled that at this time Ho Chi Minh and his colleagues maintained the façade of being a purely United
Front Nationalist movement and soft-pedaled their Communist connections. In any event, with the collapse of the
Viet Minh pretenses to administration in Saigon and Hué,
and with the arrival of two French divisions in Tonkin, events
rapidly drew to the breaking point. Full-scale hostilities began with a Viet Minh surprise attack on the French in Hanoi
on December 19, 1946. As Bernard B. Fall succinctly put it,
"the French forces sent to Indochina were too strong for
France to resist the temptation of using them; yet not strong
enough to keep the Viet Minh from trying to solve the whole
political problem by throwing the French into the sea." [24]
    With their heavier gunpower and uncontested air suprem-
acy the French at first were optimistic and thought that they
were in for a "police operation" which could shortly be

mopped up. After all, had not their forces in 1930 destroyed the starving peasants of the "Xo-Viet Nghe-An"? Before the French forces the Viet Minh fled to the mountains north of Hanoi. In the fall of 1947 a French expeditionary force almost captured Ho Chi Minh himself. The Viet Minh command correctly assessed its situation as an example of Mao Tse-tung's concept of protracted war. The Viet Minh commander, General Giap, late in 1950 had patterned the three-phase strategy by which he would fight the war: retreat and defense; equilibrium and mopping up of French posts in Viet Minh-held areas; and then a general counteroffensive. Basically his *"Guerre Mobile"* was a war of attrition which would be climaxed by a counteroffensive and the taking of Hanoi in 1951.[25]

It must be remembered that this was still a colonial war of Vietnamese nationalism seeking to wrest independence from the French. Yet by now the principles of strategy on the Viet Minh side were clearly of Communist origin. Giap's three concepts of defense, equilibrium and offense stemmed directly from the writings of Mao Tse-tung. He and Ho Chi Minh were likewise guided in their estimate of the situation and the operations requisite to victory by the Leninist concept of revolution: that revolutions could be won by opportunism rather than by uncompromising consistency with abstract principles; and that, above all, revolution would take place in two stages. The Communist revolution could occur only after a Nationalist revolution had prepared the way by preparing the necessary conditions precedent, including the overthrow of the colonial regime and the establishment of an indigenous government. After the bourgeois Nationalist coup d'état had prepared the way, the Communists would come in with the triumphant and final second stage Socialist revolution.

Ho Chi Minh made this very clear in a statement to two

correspondents of the Italian Communist party paper *Unitá,* published in that journal on July 1, 1959, when he said

. . . we [the Lao Dong (Communist) Party] are building socialism in Viet Nam. We are building it, however, only in half of the country, while in the other half, we must still bring to a conclusion the democratic-bourgeois and anti-imperialist revolution. Actually, our party must now accomplish, contemporaneously, two different revolutions, in the north and in the south. This is one of the most characteristic traits of our struggle.[26]

And all of this coincided with the taking of mainland China by Mao Tse-tung.

CHAPTER X

"Wars of National Liberation": The Franco-Communist War in Viet Nam, 1950–1954

> In this type of war there is really no enemy territory — land is unimportant. And so the people, for whom we are really fighting, are the ones who often must suffer.*

1.

1950 THEREFORE BECOMES a watershed point in the history of the war in Indochina. Prior to that time it had been a straight limited war of a colonial character, nationalist natives seeking to become independent of the metropolitan European power. Now, however, with Communism triumphant in all of China save Taiwan, the situation radically altered. It became parallel to the situation of the Eastern European states contiguous to Soviet power. The sanctuary in South China, which heretofore had been merely a haven for a handful of refugees, now became a sanctuary on the order of that in Manchuria and Siberia during the Korean War which had just opened. It provided the guns from which, as Mao Tse-tung had proclaimed, blossoms power: the guns of Dien Bien Phu.

It is from this climactic date of 1950 that the war in Viet

* Letter to the author from Colonel Leo Dulacki, G–2, Third Marine Amphibious Force, Da Nang, January 9, 1966.

Nam insensibly changed its character. Very quickly the Indochinese party which had been dissolved in 1945 as a concession to the simple "united front" strategy was reconstituted in 1951 as the Lao Dong Party.[1] The tactics and strategy of the Viet Minh now began more openly to wear the Communist integument of "wars of national liberation."

2.

The techniques of the Viet Minh were intelligent and skillful. They provided a place for everyone to serve, whether it was a peasant coolie working as a porter to maintain the logistic system of the guerrilla forces or the puppet "Emperor" Bao Dai, who for a while accepted an appointment by Ho Chi Minh as "Supreme Adviser."

The Viet Minh also won popularity by their campaign against illiteracy. This, in a country where 80 per cent of the population was illiterate, meant a boon to the majority of the people. Furthermore, from the Communist point of view it gave the Viet Minh a direct channel for political indoctrination. Finally, the Viet Minh used the instrument of land reform as a powerful lever upon the peasant population to win their loyalty and support or to intimidate them by terror. Private land was confiscated and distributed to the tenant farmers. The landowners were executed or imprisoned. In the calculated wave of terror of the Communist Land Reform Campaign it is estimated that 100,000 people were killed.[2]

The DRV established military commands in six interzones and at each administrative level committees of resistance and administration were set up. These committees were empowered to recruit local militia organized in the so-called "popular troops." At the apex of the pyramid was the regular army — the "liberation army." Every element of the popu-

lation was organized. Such was the political and social structure of the Communist Viet Minh, supported by China,
against whom the French were still fighting a "colonial war."

Thus by 1950 stood the Viet Minh, led by a legendary
figure in the person of Ho Chi Minh, possessed of a time-
tested philosophy of revolution inherited from Lenin, a concept of strategy and tactics vindicated by Mao Tse-tung, and
now standing contiguous to a military base of supply in South
Communist China. Although the wispy little figures in the
black pajamas never seemed to be drawn to pitched battles,
they were everywhere throughout the Tonkin and in increasing numbers in Cochin-China. In between lay the *Chaine
Annemite* with its inhospitable Montagnards, who had no
love for Vietnamese, either from north or south. It was a war
approaching the second phase in Giap's calculation of equilibrium. It was a war aptly described by the French colonel
who briefed General Mark Clark (with the author serving
as interpreter) in a school for military noncoms near Hanoi
in 1953. He said, *"Mon Général, nous controlons l'asphalte;
ils controlent la boue."* — We control the asphalt; they control the mud. The colonel added, thoughtfully, "And during the night the Viet Minh control both."

3.

Against this adversary the French had had imposed, or
imposed upon themselves, formidable obstacles. In the first
place they were white. They came of an alien and con-
quering race whose seat of power was 7000 miles distant from
the rice paddies, mountains and jungles of Viet Nam. They
were the daguerreotype picture of a nineteenth-century
colonial power which, as we have seen, operated Indochina
as fief for the benefit of the mother country. Furthermore,
and this was fundamental to the loss of the war by the

French, they had never at any time given any completely trustworthy assurance that Viet Nam, or Laos, or Cambodia would in truth be set free.

This was in particular of importance in Viet Nam, since Laotians did not much care anyway, and in the case of the Cambodians, to that united, homogeneous people, loyal to their king, eventual independence seemed in fact assured. Repeated observers, of whom the most illustrious was President Eisenhower, have remarked with puzzlement on the inability of the French to concede independence to Viet Nam.[3] As President Eisenhower was later to write:

> It was almost impossible to make the average Vietnamese peasant realize that the French, under whose rule his people had lived for some eighty years, were really fighting in the cause of freedom, while the Vietminh, people of their own ethnic origins, were fighting on the side of slavery. It was generally conceded that had elections been held, Ho Chi Minh would have been elected Premier. Unhappily, the situation was exacerbated by the almost total lack of leadership displayed by the Vietnamese Chief of State, Bao Dai, who, while nominally the head of that nation, chose to spend the bulk of his time in the spas of Europe rather than in his own land leading his armies against those of Communism.[4]

Even General Ely, the last Commander in Chief and Commissioner General in Indochina, was to write in his memoirs that the Viet Minh had "the sole privilege of fighting for the people's freedom and independence."[5]

4.

In addition to the fact that they were an alien suzerain power (which had been defeated both in Europe and in Asia in World War II), were white, were colonialists of the nineteenth-century tradition, and had failed to convince anyone of any real intent to grant independence to Viet Nam, the French committed the culminating political folly of devising an incubus in the person of the "Chief of State," Bao Dai. The illusion that this professional puppet could inspire devotion on the part of the Vietnamese population was a myth contrived by the "Old Indochina Hands," the types who would sit at the Cercle Sportif in Saigon and harp back to "the good old days" when the luxury train ran regularly between Saigon and Hanoi and they could partake of their afternoon opium or mistresses with absolute ease.

Bao Dai became Emperor of Viet Nam at the age of twelve, in 1925, on the death of his father, the Emperor Khai Dinh. However, he did not formally ascend the throne until 1932, after he had completed his education in France. During this last phase of the colonial period Bao Dai was nothing more than a façade for the French colonial administration. Facile as a chameleon, he was quick to change his colors after the fall of France and the arrival of the Japanese in Indochina. On March 11, 1945, he declared Viet Nam "independent" under Japanese protection and formed a so-called government at Hué. This period of "independence," Japanese-style, was short-lived as the misfortunes of war pressed inexorably upon the Japanese. Following their defeat Bao Dai abdicated in August 1945 in favor of the People's Democratic Government of Ho Chi Minh, to whom he was attached briefly as "Supreme Adviser," and later went to Hong Kong to live at greater ease.

The French began negotiations with Bao Dai in Hong Kong in the summer of 1947. These continued until March 1949 when by agreement Viet Nam was made an Associated State in the French Union with Bao Dai as Chief of State. (Here it may be noted that at this time Ngo Dinh Diem rejected both Bao Dai and Ho Chi Minh, demanding independence for Viet Nam on the basis of commonwealth status as recently achieved by India and Pakistan.)[6] The agreement of March 8, 1949 with Bao Dai provided for a Vietnamese cabinet to have charge of internal affairs and the administration of a national army under French command — but Paris was to keep direct control of foreign policy, maintain military bases and extraterritorial courts for Frenchmen, and retain also a special place for French advisers and the French language. Such was the "Declaration of Independence" of March 8, 1949.

In a recent lecture at the U.S. Naval War College (December 9, 1965) the distinguished historian of the wars in Viet Nam, Dr. Bernard B. Fall, made extensive quotations from an issue of *Time* magazine. One of the quotes ran as follows: "The French insist that the military problem is the number one problem and that Western men and arms must lick it. Given sufficient U.S. equipment up to $150 million or more a year, they think they can crush Ho Chi Minh within three years." * Dr. Fall went on to quote from *Time*:

> It is Bao Dai's mission, and the U.S.-French hope, to rally his countrymen to the anti-Communist camp of the West. In this undertaking he needs time. "Nothing can be done overnight," he says. He needs time to organize an effective native government, train an army and militia that can restore order in the villages, win over the doubting fence-sitters among the intelligentsia. Besides a military shield, he also needs a display of winning strength and patient understanding by his Western allies.

The cover picture on this issue of *Time* magazine, dated May 29, 1950, was that of Bao Dai.[7]

The author, as Chargé d'Affaires of the United States in Saigon during one-third of the time he spent in Viet Nam,

---

* Professor Fall wryly notes that generals and politicians have a fondess for "three-year" estimates of future victory. A lesser time limit would be militarily foolhardy; a longer period politically impossible.

had many opportunities to meet and study Bao Dai. He even once translated into French for Bao Dai a speech by Vice President Nixon, and escorted Adlai Stevenson to lunch with the "Emperor" in what Stevenson called "that Sears Roebuck Palace" at Ban Me Thuot. The French were wholly committed to the Bao Dai expedient; and even such an experienced observer as Malcolm MacDonald, the British Commissioner General at Singapore, claimed that he was the indispensable man "because he had the courage to wait."

Bao Dai had no courage except in ambushing tigers and seducing women. He was, however, highly intelligent and he knew how to wait. He had, in fact, been on every side of every fence in Viet Nam since he was twelve years old and always, according to his lights, on the winning side. His final triumph just before his last return to France was to sell the concession for the police forces of Saigon-Cholon to the gangster band, the Binh Xuyen. From this deal, which was equivalent to the City of Chicago in the days of Al Capone having turned over its police forces to that gangster in return for a multi-million-dollar bribe, the absentee Emperor actually stowed away some 49 million francs in his personal airplane when he departed Saigon for Cannes.[8]

Such was the symbol of "independence" for which the Vietnamese were supposed to fight and bleed and die against the nationalist forces of Ho Chi Minh.

5.

The war continued, as President Eisenhower has noted:

The picture at the time of my inauguration indicated the growing size and importance of the war. The French had deployed, at that time, forces numbering half a million men under arms. During the seven years of fighting, casualties had totaled 132,000 wounded and 48,000 killed. In 1952, the French lost more officers than were graduated that year from its Military College, Saint Cyr, and in prosecuting the war, the French had spent more than $3.5 billion out of their war-damaged economy. But the French had still not unequivocally promised to the Associated States the right of self-determination.[9]

French High Commissioners and Commanders in Chief came and went. Even the great Marshal De Lattre de Tassigny, the French MacArthur, with all his personal magnetism, energy and drive, was not able to upset that ominous equilibrium, postulated by his adversary, Giap, in his over-all strategy. De Lattre died of cancer on January 11, 1952, and was replaced by General Raoul Salan, "The Mandarin." The author well remembers General Salan, reportedly the most decorated officer in the French Army, standing in the reviewing stand in Saigon and proudly watching his half-Laotian natural son, a lieutenant in the Armée Coloniale, leading his company down the avenue. Salan himself went down a longer and more sinuous road, leading the revolt against France in Algiers. He now is under a penalty of life imprisonment at the Fortress of Tulle.

On May 19, 1953, Salan was replaced as Commander in Chief by General Henri Navarre. Most of his long military career had been spent in the Intelligence. He was lucid, cold, clear, and gave the impression of being faintly sardonic. He had also achieved the knack which only Frenchmen can master of continuously smoking a cigarette half made of an ash which trembles but never falls. Unlike the haughty De Lattre or the sly Salan, or the bull-like Breton Commander in Tonkin, General Cogny, Navarre always stood at the interminable military parades taking the salute with his neat pot stomach well out in front and his shoulders caved in. It was to Navarre that the hard-pressed politicians of the Fourth Republic had entrusted the task of so contriving a favorable military situation that ultimately *la sale guerre* could be brought to a negotiated conclusion. In the words of General Ely:

> His objective, which incidentally was in conformity with the instructions he had received, was to create military conditions which would allow the Government to find a satisfactory and honorable political solution to the Indochina problem. In short, it was a question of showing the Viet Minh that they had no chance of conquering us by force of arms, and that they must therefore accept a negotiated settlement.[10]

It is curious how the pronouncements of statesmen and military commanders have a repetitive ring . . .

The Navarre plan had been bequeathed to him by his predecessor, General Salan. The Viet Minh in their fifth military region in North Annam, separated from Tonkin by a range of mountains, would be mopped up by "Operation Atlante." The French would then entice the enemy's battle force to disaster as the troops of Salan under Brigadier Gilles had wiped out the encircling human waves of Viet Minh at Na San the year before.

The site for this intended massacre of the enemy was remote, some 200 air miles west-northwest of Hanoi in a mountain valley near the border of Laos called Muong Theng, in the country of the Thai. In the center of this valley upon its main river stood a village called Dien Bien Phu. "Dien" in Vietnamese means big, "Bien" — a frontier, and "Phu" — an administrative center. So in all Dien Bien Phu, whose name later became laden with far more doomful meaning, meant "the big administrative center on the frontier." [11] Because of its proximity to Laos, Navarre was also convinced that a strong entrenched camp at Dien Bien Phu would block a Viet Minh thrust toward the royal capital of Luang Prabang. But his main purpose was to make of Dien Bien Phu a meatchopper for the Viet Minh.

On November 20, 1953, Navarre commenced the operation at Dien Bien Phu. On the forenoon of that day 3000 French parachutists descended on the valley, including the Sixth Parachute Battalion under Bigéard and the First Paratroops under Bréchignac. Swiftly a landing strip was prepared and the French Air Force Dakotas (C–47s) brought in the tons of equipment necessary for a fortified camp to be garrisoned by 11,000 troops.

On November 25, the French Intelligence intercept service in Hanoi had taken the radio orders which Giap had issued to the 308th, 312th, and the 351st divisions. French Intelligence believed that the 316th Division, which was already en route, would reach Dien Bien Phu by December 6th. The 308th would be in place by the 24th, the 351st Heavy Division about the 26th and the 312th about the 28th.[12] This, according to the Salan-Navarre Plan, was just what the French wanted: an opportunity decisively to whip the enemy with the superior firepower of the French heavy artillery and the uncontested French Air Force. Furthermore, according to the calculations of the French staff, "the concentration of four Viet Minh divisions was also regarded as a utopian project. To keep fifty thousand combat troops alive, fifty thousand coolies would have to carry rice incessantly, material and ammunition would have to be brought up along communication lines where the convoys would be surprised and destroyed by the Air Force."[13] So far everything was going according to plan. It was also going according to the plan of Vo Nguyen Giap.

It is not intended here to recapitulate the story of the battle of Dien Bien Phu. The account has already brilliantly been made by Colonel Jules Roy in his book, *The Battle of Dien Bien Phu,* and by other military writers. It is essential only to this account to realize that once more a limited war had limitless results; that the French in General Navarre had made a massive military mistake which would only be exceeded in its consequences by the fact that Dien Bien Phu became the most important political battle of the twentieth century.

As an experienced Intelligence officer, General Navarre had ample Intelligence. Intercepts indicated that by March 10 there were 70,000 Viet Minh troops surrounding Dien Bien Phu. These included twenty-seven infantry battalions, twenty 105 mm. guns, eighteen 75 mm. guns, eighty 37 mm. guns and one hundred 12.7 antiaircraft guns, not counting the mortars. There were 5000 rounds of 75 mm. ammunition, 15,000 rounds of 105 mm. shells, 44,000 rounds of 37 mm. antiaircraft shells and 24,000 shells for the mortars. The supply of food had reached to 70 tons a day. This did not seem much like the opportunity afforded at Na San unless, as Lieutenant Colonel Gaucher, who was soon to be killed at Dien Bien Phu, pointed out, the "105 mm. guns were made of wood." [14]

As for the supposed requirement of 50,000 coolies a day to carry rice to the besiegers of the garrison, intercept at Christmas time revealed that 2000 bicycles were on their way toward Dien Bien Phu. Specially rigged, each bicycle could carry up to 500 pounds of rice or munitions, more per bicycle than an elephant could carry. As for the guns, they were dragged by trucks at night and hidden up in camouflaged revetments by day. Nevertheless, despite the evidence of the Intelligence, Navarre, the Intelligence officer, drew the wrong conclusions — or at least he preferred to ignore the evidence. This was not a case as in Korea of the commanding general being deceived by faulty intelligence, although in the cases of both MacArthur and Navarre wishful thinking undoubtedly had its play.

The battle began on the morning of March 13 and continued with heavy artillery pounding and human wave assaults launched from an extensive network of trenches. The commander of the French artillery at Dien Bien Phu, Colonel Piroth, who had boasted that his 155 mm. guns would quickly knock out any Viet Minh artillery by accurate counter-battery fire, went to his bunk, took a hand grenade, placed it next to his heart and pulled the pin.[15]

The deluge of shells continued to rain on the entrenched camp. Three days after the beginning of the attack, one of the French strong points, Gabrielle, fell to the Viet Minh who rapidly installed antiaircraft batteries and mortars which placed the airstrip, the lifeline of Dien Bien Phu, under interdiction except for hazardous night landings. "Three days after the beginning of the attack, and contrary to all expectations, Dien Bien Phu had been deprived of its principal support." [16]

The author has before him the battle map of Dien Bien Phu which was on the wall of his Embassy office in Saigon during the long agony of that conflict. The French strongpoints were romantically named after the girl friends of their commanders. These included Gabrielle, the most northerly stronghold and the first to fall; Anne-Marie; Béatrice; Huguette; Dominique; Françoise; Claudine; Eliane; and finally far to the south, Isabelle, from which the last attempt to sortie by the Foreign Legion was frustrated. As Colonel Roy has written, "The glory of Dien Bien Phu . . . was that of fighting on the bloodiest dunghill in Asia, in the name of the West and for the love of the pretty girls who had given their names to the peaks." [17]

Each day the area grew smaller; each day the lines of trenches crept closer to the peaks with the nostalgic names. Each night the defenders of the fortress heard the Viet Minh sappers busily tunneling under their strong points. As for the airstrip, it now was useless. The only means of supply of men, munitions and the essential *vinogel* or red Algerian wine was by airdrop and much of this cargo, human and otherwise, fell within the Viet Minh lines. It became apparent to everyone that only a miracle could save Dien Bien Phu.

6.

On February 18, 1954, the Berlin Conference came to an end with only one conclusion: To meet at Geneva on April 26 to discuss the problems of Korea and Indochina. Thus the agony at Dien Bien Phu had as a broader backdrop the green baize of the negotiating table at the Palais des Nations. On March 20, 1954, the chairman of the French Joint Chiefs of Staff, General Paul Ely, arrived in Washington to work out details for increased American support of the French effort in Viet Nam. He was received by President Eisenhower who in Ely's words ordered Admiral Radford, the Chairman of the U.S. Joint Chiefs, "to furnish us, on a priority basis, everything we asked for, in order to save the entrenched camp." [18] When General Ely called on Secretary of State Dulles he

> made clear to him that in the views of the French Government and French Command a military solution to the Indochinese conflict at reasonable cost and on reasonable terms did not seem possible, and that it was advisable to seek a political solution to the problem.[19]

In Secretary Dulles' memorandum to President Eisenhower he noted that he

> did, however, think it appropriate to remind our French friends that if the United States sent its flag and its own military establishment — land, sea, or air — into the Indo-China war, then the prestige of the United States would be engaged to a point where we would want to have a success. We could not afford thus to engage the prestige of the United States and suffer a defeat which would have worldwide repercussions.[20]

General Ely quoted the Secretary more forcefully: "The United States would then view such a conflict, in which their forces would be so directly involved, as calling for nothing short of total victory." [21]

Although in these talks the possibility of American intervention was considered only in the hypothesis of Chinese aerial action in Indochina,[22] Admiral Radford, according to Ely, privately discussed with him the possibility of a French request for U.S. Air Force intervention at Dien Bien Phu, using B–29's stationed at Clark Field in the Philippines.[23] Neither Admiral Radford nor General Ely felt that such an intervention would lead to general war. When Ely returned to Paris March 27 he reported to the Ministers of Defense, Pleven, and Foreign Affairs, Bidault. The Government was interested. It dispatched Colonel Brohon, General Ely's aide-de-camp, to outline the proposal which later became dubbed "Operation Vautour" (Vulture) to General Navarre, whom he saw on April 2 in Hanoi. Brohon returned to Paris April 4, bringing "an unenthusiastic response from the Commander in Chief," on the ground that "it involved too great a risk of Chinese aerial reaction." The Commander in Chief soon changed his mind. In fact his telegram was received by General Ely on April 4, the day of Colonel Brohon's return. Now Navarre made a definite request for the earliest possible intervention by American aircraft at Dien Bien Phu.[24]

There has been much speculation as to whether the contemplated American attack would have been nuclear in character. Colonel Roy quotes Colonel Brohon as telling General Navarre that A-bombs were indeed involved.[25] In fact, General Curtis LeMay, then Chief of SAC, informed the author at Omaha in May 1957 that indeed he had drawn up a plan for the tactical nuclear bombardment of Dien Bien Phu. Asked what would happen to the French garrison, LeMay calmly replied, "Well, I guess they'd have got it too." General Ely insists that despite the fact that the use of

nuclear weapons may have been discussed from time to time,
"the idea of using them in the battle of Dien Bien Phu could
not withstand even a summary examination. That would
without a doubt have torpedoed the Geneva negotiation and
thrown the world into an unroar." * 26

In this estimate of the political situation General Ely was
fundamentally right.

7.

However, the issue never came to the test. It was against
the background of two difficult certainties — the convocation
of the Geneva Conference on April 26 and the apparent in-
evitability of defeat at Dien Bien Phu — that President
Eisenhower and Secretary Dulles began to hammer out the
outlines of a Southeast Asia Pact. The immediate catalyst
was the French request for U.S. intervention at Dien Bien
Phu. However, the President and the Secretary felt unwilling
for the United States to go in without allies. On April 4
President Eisenhower wrote Prime Minister Churchill sug-
gesting

> the establishment of a new, ad hoc grouping or coalition
> composed of nations which have a vital concern in the check-

---

* On the point of contingent planning for possible U.S. air intervention
at Dien Bien Phu, Admiral Arthur W. Radford has written the author (January 7, 1966) as follows:

> I am familiar with General Ely's memoirs — as a matter of fact I
> have a copy on my desk right now. His statements, of course, are based
> on French planning, but do not represent U.S. thinking.
> I am not sure that my recollections are accurate and I could only
> find out with great difficulty by digging back in the files. However, as
> I recall such plans as were probably made were contingent plans and
> they were probably made by the services individually as a precautionary
> measure. As far as the President, the Secretary of Defense and the JCS
> were concerned, no orders were ever issued to make detailed plans —
> this is as I recall it.
> I would imagine that plans were made for both contingencies as you
> suppose. I certainly know that if we had undertaken this assignment,
> we would have taken steps to see that the actions would assure success.

ing of Communist expansion in the area. I have in mind in
addition to our two countries, France, the Associated States,
Australia, New Zealand, Thailand, and the Philippines. The
United States Government would expect to play its full part
in such a coalition . . .[27]

The British Foreign Secretary, Anthony Eden, described
the American proposal:

This was to the effect that all the countries concerned should
issue, before Geneva, a solemn declaration of their readiness
to take concerted action under Article 51 of the United Nations Charter, against the continued interference by China
in the Indochina war. We were informed that the proposed
warning would carry with it the threat of naval and air action
against the Chinese Coast and an active intervention in
Indochina itself.[28]

The author at this time was the senior American diplomatic
representative in Indochina, stationed as Chargé d'Affaires
in Saigon, but having supervisory jurisdiction over our small,
one-man diplomatic missions in Phnom Penh, Cambodia,
and Vientiane, Laos. In this situation he was privileged to
be the recipient of some exceedingly classified telegrams
which indicated that the United States was on the brink
of military intervention. In fact, some French liaison officers,
who were not privy to the Top Secret conversations held with
General Navarre and French High Commissioner de Jean,
bitterly protested to the Embassy against the "interference"
of reconnaissance aircraft from the Seventh Fleet which had
been looking over the ground at Dien Bien Phu.

The author also had the diplomatic task of acting as buffer, go-between, counselor, and interpreter (but mostly buffer) for two generals of identically opposite character and
approach. These were the French Commander, Lieutenant
General Henri Navarre, and the senior American military officer in Indochina, Major General John W. O'Daniel, who
headed the MAAG or Military Assistance Advisory Group in

Saigon. "Iron Mike" as he was either affectionately or fearfully called, was a gallant infantryman of immense personal war experience.* In fact, he so enjoyed the confidence of President Eisenhower and Admiral Radford and was so devoted to the cause of *winning* in Indochina (a concept remote from General Navarre's thinking) that he voluntarily reduced himself in rank from Lieutenant General to Major General in order not to outrank the French Commander in Chief when he took command of MAAG, Saigon.

General Navarre, who after the fall of Dien Bien Phu confided to the author that he had to himself conceded defeat after the first thirty-six hours of the battle, was intellectually indisposed to listen to the vehement demands of General O'Daniel "to do something" to relieve the beleaguered garrison at Dien Bien Phu. "Iron Mike" in fact was constantly devising plans for sending relief columns through Laos or dropping more men and matériel to interdict the Viet Minh lines of supply to the siege. However, the two generals never saw eye to eye and perhaps it was just as well that the Chargé d'Affaires should act as interpreter as neither officer understood the other's language, both literally and figuratively. The author once remarked to a friend that to expect Navarre and O'Daniel to work in unison was about as optimistic as to harness a water buffalo and a gazelle to pull a plow through a Vietnamese rice paddy.

President Eisenhower phrased it more delicately in his memoirs in a footnote to his account of "chaos in Indochina":

> General O'Daniel had outlined a plan for the relief of Dien Bien Phu involving forces available, which would make use of a parachute drop of three battalions, plus an attack from Hanoi to Dien Bien Phu by armored groups and mechanized infantry elements. Despite O'Daniel's confi-

---

* When "Iron Mike" once arrived at Tan Son Nhut airport at Saigon the author sent a Second Secretary to receive him. An hour later the young diplomat returned pale and shaking, "Rob," he said, "the General's voice sounds like ice water flowing over gravel!"

dence in his plan, he felt reluctant about submitting it directly to General Navarre in view of Navarre's sensitivities and O'Daniel's limited terms of reference as chief of the United States Military Advisory and Assistance Group (MAAG). Therefore he passed it on to our chargé d'affaires, Mr. McClintock, who spoke to the French Commissioner General, M. Maurice de Jean. The plan was considered but never attempted by the French high command.[29]

While the United States, French and British governments secretly debated the pros and cons of intervention at Dien Bien Phu, either unilaterally by the United States, or as desired by President Eisenhower in concert with other allies, the last agonies of the fortress drew to their close. It is clear from the record [30] that Churchill and Eden were opposed to any allied intervention at this hour when the clock stood at 59 minutes to midnight.

Dien Bien Phu fell on May 7 and the great and gallant subordinates, the indomitable Centurions, Langlais, Bréchignac, Bigéard, went into the annals of the other great and gallant soldiers of history. As for Brigadier General de Castries, the commander of the entrenched camp, the kindest epitaph was pronounced by Colonel Langlais before a court of inquiry. When asked what function did Brigadier de Castries perform, Langlais replied with a touch of humor, "He transmitted our messages to Hanoi." [31] After the first bombardment began on March 13 until the end on May 7 de Castries, the titular commander, never left his dugout.

8.

On June 18 Pierre Mendès-France replaced Joseph Laniel as Prime Minister of France. Sensing the revulsion of his people and correctly drawing conclusions as to the political nature of the battle of Dien Bien Phu, the new Prime Minister gave himself an ultimatum: he announced that he would secure a peace in Indochina by July 20. Surely never has a major diplomatic conference been given such a self-imposed time limit by a principal party whose side has just suffered a major defeat. However, the dynamism of Mendès-France, the skill of his principal negotiator, Ambassador Chauvel, and the experience in diplomacy of the British Foreign Secretary and the American Under Secretary of State, General Bedell Smith, all contributed to the result. Furthermore, the Viet Minh, although victorious at Dien Bien Phu, still had a long road to go; nor had Mao Tse-tung disregarded the lessons he had learned at the hands of the Americans in the war in Korea. And behind all the statesmen and diplomats, as Eden pointed out in his memoirs, was the deterrent power of the hydrogen bomb.[32]

Late in the afternoon of July 20, Mendès-France and the Viet Minh delegate announced that they had reached an agreement on a line of partition which was to be a river just south of the 17th parallel. In the two Viet Nams, north and south, elections would not be held until July 1956. There were detailed provisions for the withdrawal of the armed forces from both North and South Viet Nam. A cease-fire would go into effect throughout Indochina. The kingdoms of Laos and Cambodia became in fact independent. Three International Control Commissions composed of representatives of India, Poland, and Canada would supervise the agreements. However, one of the parties to the conflict, the State of South Viet Nam, refused to sign the Geneva agreement, nor did its silent partner, the United States.* Thus the French war in Indochina had ended.

---

* The United States did, however, make a unilateral declaration at the concluding plenary session of the Geneva Conference on July 21, 1954. In taking note of the agreements just signed, the U.S. Government declared that it would refrain from the threat or the use of force to disturb them, and that "it would view any renewal of the aggression in violation of the aforesaid agreements with grave concern and as seriously threatening international peace and security." [33]

9.

As suggested above, the watershed date is 1950, between the time when the isolated war of the Viet Minh against their colonial masters, the French, changed into a limited war of the Viet Minh against the French but with outside intervention.

1949–50 were the years when Communist power took over mainland China. This provided the essential sanctuary and base for the supply of the heavy weapons which made Giap victorious at Dien Bien Phu. Had it not been for the 105 mm. gun-howitzers, the 75 mm. artillery and the 37 mm. antiaircraft guns, all of the 70,000 troops which Giap massed around Dien Bien Phu would have been unavailing against the French 155's and the French Air Force. It was Red China's aid in these artillery weapons, plus Giap's skill as a master logistician-cum-tactician which spelled out victory for the Viet Minh at Dien Bien Phu.

On the side of the West the United States, which had been locked in desperate war against the Communists in Korea, was quick to realize that France needed assistance if it were to stem the tide now that the Asiatic mainland in China had gone into the Communist camp. The United States also at that time was seeking to sustain France by budgetary support and by economic aid under the Marshall Plan and the NATO alliance. One of the great concerns of the period proved later to be the chimera of EDC — The European Defense Community — so dear to the heart of Foster Dulles, and in this Community France would have played a major role. Thus American policy both in the Atlantic and Pacific was linked with the destinies of France, and concerns for the defense of Europe swayed Washington's decisions on the defense of Southeast Asia.

The decision was made in the Truman Administration and

followed through the first part of the Eisenhower Administration, to conduct the holding action in Indochina by the use of surrogate forces — once more one of the characteristics of twentieth-century limited war. These forces from the American point of view were the French Expeditionary Corps and the newly organized South Vietnamese Army, then called the Army of Viet Nam. However, in this endeavor the Americans came up constantly against the thorny nettle of French pride, sensitivity, and suspicion.

It is not necessary to read the memoirs of Generals Navarre and Ely to see how deeply distrustful they were of their American counterparts and for that matter all the American community in Indochina. Navarre was obsessed with suspicions "about the interference of certain American businessmen who, as he said, made no secret of their eagerness to divert toward America a portion of the flow of trade necessary to the Indochina economy";[34] while Ely complained to Admiral Radford that "representatives of the American Government, even at a high level, often conducted themselves, especially in overseas territories of French influence, as if they wanted to supplant us politically and economically." [35] In Saigon both Generals Salan and Navarre and later General Ely constantly evinced to the author their insistence that American aid should be given "no strings attached" in any quantity desired by the French High Command and without any American control over its use by that command. As for the concept of Americans wishing to train Indochinese in more up-to-date methods of warfare — that was anathema. French pride is prickly.

These attitudes are understandable, although perhaps not praiseworthy. The French were fighting an endless war in an endless sea of mud for an always elusory victory. Furthermore, most of these generals, some of them alumni of German prisoner of war camps, had themselves never won a battle. They were sore.

With the change of events following Dien Bien Phu and the Geneva Conference there was an obvious need for a change in American policy. As the author wrote in a memorandum while serving as the Chairman of an Interdepartmental Working Group to formulate a new policy for postarmistice Indochina, "fundamentally U.S. policy toward Indochina should be determined by what is in our national interest in Southeast Asia. U.S. policy toward France should be determined by what is in our national interest in Europe. Our policies thus far have failed because we tried to hit two birds with one stone and missed both." [36]

10.

In a Task Force brought together in August 1954 to recommend to the Secretary of State and President "a U.S. policy toward Indochina following the Geneva cease-fire agreements which will preserve the integrity and independence of Laos, Cambodia, and Viet Nam in order that they might form a barrier to further Communist encroachment in Southeast Asia," the following recommendations were made and approved by the White House:

1. The U.S. should furnish direct, adequate economic, financial and military assistance to the three countries of Indochina. However, this assistance should be conditioned upon performance by the three countries in instituting needed reforms and carrying them out if necessary with U.S. or other assistance. The corollary to the policy of direct aid is the requirement to renegotiate with France the existing instruments which now channel U.S. aid for Indochina, both military and financial, exclusively through French hands.

2. The three Indochinese states should receive guarantees of their territorial and political integrity from an eventual Southeast Asia collective defense system. Initially, however, the three countries should not adhere to the formal collective

defense treaty but should benefit by its provisions as does Western Germany under the NATO pact. Cambodia, Laos and Free Viet Nam should be informed by the signatories of the new defense treaty that their integrity is guaranteed by that treaty."

This policy recommendation was sent to the Secretary of State on August 12, 1954. A telegram signed by Secretary Dulles was dispatched on August 18 to Ambassador Dillon in Paris instructing him to inform Prime Minister Mendès-France that U.S. aid in Indochina would henceforth go directly to the recipient states and not through the French channel.

As for measures to be taken with South Viet Nam the author recommended:

1. Refugee and rehabilitation centers should be established to receive the evacuees from Tonkin and Northern Annam to insure that this mass of displaced persons would not become the seed-bed for further Communist penetration.

2. A practical and immediate land reform program should be adopted.

3. Fiscal reforms, including the establishment of a national bank and the creation of a new currency backed by U.S. budgetary support, should be instituted.

4. A government of national union should be created.

5. A constituent assembly should be convoked.

6. The dethronement of Bao Dai should be accomplished forthwith and the crown lands reverting to the state should be used either for land reform or refugee resettlement.

7. There should be immediate reconstruction of the Vietnamese National Army. As a corollary to this the United States should negotiate a new MDAP bilateral agreement with Viet Nam which would provide for a permanent U.S. training mission.

8. A new policy of U.S. direct aid to Viet Nam, no longer "operating through a French key hole and subject to a French veto," should be established.[37]

In retrospect, although the memorandum proposing these steps has long since found oblivion in the archives, it is perhaps rewarding to note that the reforms proposed have been adopted. Yet in concluding this account of the French war in Indochina and before attempting to discern the web which history weaves of the future, it is sobering to read the caution, "many observers feel that the prospects for political stability in South Viet Nam are particularly bleak since societal factors which contributed to the success of the Viet Minh in the colonial period have, for the most part, not been changed." [38]

11.

As in the case of other limited wars which we have studied, such as the civil war in Greece and the war in Korea, the limited war in Viet Nam had almost unlimited consequences.

First of all, there were the gigantic derivations from Dien Bien Phu. The French, once they had faced up to the consequences of this defeat, applied their Cartesian logic with rigorous and intelligent discipline. It was the consequence of Dien Bien Phu which led to the rapid and orderly liberation of the French Empire in Africa, with the notable exception of Algeria. Here the defeated Centurions made their last stand, with consequences which almost destroyed France. Jouhaud, Chassin, Salan, Cogny, Gambiez: all were generals of the Indochinese war and some of them, with the tenacity of desperation and the desperation of despair, sought to retrieve in Algeria what they had lost in Viet Nam. When military victory against the rebels was almost in sight it was De Gaulle who had the greatness to intervene and, in "losing" the Algerian Department of France, saved France itself.

Once more in studying the characteristics of the limited war in Viet Nam, familiar identifications spring forth. First of all, there was widespread use of surrogate forces. The French Union troops were from the Metropole but principally from the armies of the Empire. A major portion of the forces fighting under the tricolor were Vietnamese themselves (indeed, half the garrison at Dien Bien Phu was Vietnamese). There were also troops of the Armée Coloniale: Spahis and Goums from Morocco, Senegalese and the variegated forces of the Foreign Legion. * The United States in backing the French effort in Indochina used the entire apparatus of the French Union forces as surrogate soldiers. On the other hand, the Chinese Communists in backing the Viet Minh used the entire military apparatus of the Viet Minh as surrogates against the French.

Militarily, the French were bogged down by too-heavy equipment. Although they had unlimited use of air power and controlled the seas surrounding Indochina, on land their reliance on wheeled transport made them static because of the prevalence of mud over asphalt, and they found themselves in fixed positions confronting a mobile enemy. This left the initiative to General Giap. As the French Colonel had told General Clark, "we control the asphalt, but they control the mud." Furthermore, as in the war in Korea, the coolie with the A-frame, or in the case of the Viet-Minh, the bicycle laden with 500 pounds of rice or ammunition, equaled all the resources of modern military logistics. Once more human muscle many times multiplied and sustained by hearts that had a revolutionary fervor equaled the energy stored in petrol and made mobile through machines.

In the war in Viet Nam, as in other limited wars, there

---

* Colonel Roy reports, "since it had begun, the Indochinese War had killed 3 generals, 8 colonels, 18 lieutenant colonels, 69 majors, 341 captains, 1,140 lieutenants, 3,683 NCO's, and 6,008 soldiers of French nationality; 12,019 Legionnaires and Africans; and 14,093 natives." [39]

was respect for sanctuary on both sides. South China was, after 1950, the great source of supply for the Viet Minh. It was U.S.-manufactured 105 mm. guns captured by the Chinese Communists from the forces of Chiang Kai-shek which spelled the difference between stalemate and victory for General Giap at Dien Bien Phu. On the other hand, Communist air and naval power did not seek to challenge the French Air Force or the French Navy and therefore there was sanctuary for the French both in the air and at sea. On the rivers of Indochina, however, the naval war was another story.[40]

Unlike most of the limited wars which have formed the subject of this study, the war in Indochina was not brought to the United Nations. However, a form of international control was established by the Geneva agreements in the International Control Commissions set up for Laos, Cambodia, and Viet Nam and staffed by representatives of India, Canada, and Poland.

As indicated above, the war in Viet Nam metamorphosed from a colonial limited war for independence to a "war of national liberation."

French talk of "independence" was never really credible, either to the Viet Minh or to the "loyal" Vietnamese. The contrast between an authentic nationalist in the person of Ho Chi Minh and the professional puppet emperor, Bao Dai, was pitilessly stark. Furthermore, as Ho Chi Minh continued his struggle for the independence of Viet Nam his price became higher. Ho had traveled a long way from the eight modest points he vainly sought to present to the Peace Conference at Versailles, to his demands for dominion status at the Fontainebleau Conference, to his warning to the Americans in 1945 that "if the U.N. should forget its solemn promise and if it does not give independence to Indochina, we shall continue to fight until we get it." And there is no reason to doubt that the aim of Ho Chi Minh is still an independent, unified, and Communist Viet Nam.

As the war in Viet Nam became a civil war with outside intervention (another of the characteristics of twentieth-century limited war) the strategic aims broadened out. As suggested in a preceding chapter, the purpose of Communist China was dominance. This time dominance of the Straits which link the Pacific and Indian Oceans. The objectives geographically were Malaysia and Indonesia; the route lay through Laos, Cambodia, and Viet Nam. Once again the land power of China would meet the sea power of the United States.

As in the case of Korea, the war in Viet Nam was a conflict which pitted Asians against Occidentals, the yellow race against the white. It was an easy dialectical transition to portray the war as one of simon-pure yellow nationalists against white "imperialists." Nor would it be easy to persuade Asian and African peoples that in fact the West was fighting to set men free. This was indeed a conflict to fit the new Communist prescription for a "war of national liberation."

It is necessary, therefore, to take a closer look at that new political invention for changing the world balance of power: the "war of national liberation."

CHAPTER XI

"Wars of National Liberation"

1.

In 1965 the Vice President of the United States, speaking before the National War College, described the Communist political invention of "wars of national liberation" as a "bold new form of aggression which could rank in military importance with the discovery of gun powder."

Thus Mr. Humphrey, perhaps by deliberate overstatement, sought to dramatize the newest, most insidious and dangerous form of Communist attack against freedom. Certainly "wars of national liberation" are as explosive as gunpowder; and it will be recalled that the inventors of gunpowder were Chinese. Yet in these times of crisis it is well to remember that the two Chinese ideographs for "crisis" are the characters for "danger" and "opportunity."

Although Mao Tse-tung had for many years sketched the anatomy of subversive war and made a clinical analysis of its three progressive stages, and the Kremlin had made its attempt to stage a civil war for strategic aims in Greece, the concept of "wars of national liberation" as a political-military technique of aggression is relatively recent. Khrushchev first enunciated it in his speech to the Communist Congress on January 6, 1961; and it was in 1961 that the twenty-second Congress outlined a twenty-year strategy of "anti-imperialist national liberation revolutions."

Although not stated, the reason for this was that the balance of power between the United States and the U.S.S.R. had made it impossible for Communism to achieve conquest by open war. They had tried and had failed in Greece and Korea. China made a warning strike in India in the high Himalayas; and both China and the U.S.S.R. gave logistic support to the Communist side in Viet Nam. Still a new technique seemed necessary if the political equilibrium of the world should be tipped in their favor. Some new means of attack had to be devised. Half a century before, Lenin had perceived that the force of nationalism could be used like gasoline to power the motor of Communism. He and his successors also saw that the conditions where Communism could most easily ingratiate itself were those conditions of economic and social disequilibrium — call it social injustice if you will — which were more prevalent in the newly emergent nations than in the old established societies. If the world balance of power were to be shifted in favor of Communism, the weak flanks of the West lay in the so-called underdeveloped countries, or, to apply a Churchillian phrase in global proportion, "the soft under-belly of the world."

2.

What are the characteristics of these countries where the conditions exist for "wars of national liberation"? Many are new nations recently emerged from colonial dominion. They are countries where the "have-nots" are many and the "haves" are few. They are countries where conditions of economic and social deprivation lead to unrest in the mass of the population, and where the bourgeois central administration becomes a target for its enemies, an obvious illustration of Lenin's concept of a two-stage revolutionary process. They are countries of massive inexperience in self-government, many with prefabricated constitutions which can only operate in politically mature societies. They are countries of honest ignorance: ignorance of how trade and finance and education and government really function; countries where Goethe's phrase has a deadly ring — "there is nothing more dangerous than ignorance in action."

These new nations are also prey to emotion. Their background in many ways disposes them to be "anti" spelled in capital letters. Probably a majority of the world's population in greater or less degree is anti-white. Most of the states of Africa, Arabia and South Asia are almost by definition anti-imperialist. Many of the emergent states have populations uniformly anti-landowner, anti-rich, anti-middle class. Most of the underdeveloped countries, if not anti the industrial nations, feel keenly that as producers of raw materials they are prey to what to them seems the whimsy of world markets.

Is there any wonder then that the great Communist powers, in facing the fact of the atomic deterrent and in formulating a new strategy for the next score of years, should have come up with the formula adopted by the twenty-second Communist Congress: that of "anti-imperialist national liberation revolutions"?

3.

The strategy having been determined, the tactics are fairly simple. Given the conditions outlined above, the explosive force of nationalism is piped through the organ of anti-feelings, most of them against the West. Since it is always easier to destroy than to build, and since Communism operates without any obligation to the truth, the task is first to eliminate the existing order, while at the same time promising Utopia to the masses who toil and fight on the marge of the mirage. This is the first of Lenin's two stages, the "bourgeois revolution." Political subversion supports, and is supported by, guerrilla warfare and terrorism. Eventually, it is expected, "wars of national liberation" will move through the classical three stages postulated by Mao Tse-tung; "imperialist, bourgeois governments" will be overthrown, and the classless Nirvana of the Communist ant hill will be achieved.*

Unfortunately for the giant Communist land powers, 70 per cent of the earth's surface is covered by sea; and the zones in which lie the countries candidate for "wars of national liberation" are in most cases adjacent to the sea. A chart of the soft under-belly of the world where lie the necessary elements for "wars of national liberation" shows how susceptible to sea power are the areas chosen for Communist aggression. (See endpaper map.) And the peoples thus threatened might keep in mind the aphorism of Samuel Eliot Morison in his recent *History of the American People* that "Sea power has never led to despotism."

To be practical about it, one might as well list the countries candidate for "wars of national liberation." Starting with Asia, we have already seen how the Communists tried and failed to win an objective of immense strategic consequence in Korea. They tried and failed in the Hukbalahap insurrection in the Philippines. They tried and failed in eight years of guerrilla jungle war in Malaya. They won the battle of Dien Bien Phu, described in the preceding chapter as the most important political battle yet fought in the twentieth

---

* This was strikingly revealed in the article by the Chinese Communist Defense Minister, Marshal Lin Piao, published in all Chinese major newspapers on September 3, 1965. He wrote, "The countryside, and the countryside alone, can provide the revolutionary bases from which the revolutionaries can go forward to final victory . . . Taking the entire globe, if North America and Western Europe can be called 'the cities of the world,' then Asia, Africa and Latin America constitute 'the rural areas of the world'." As the New York *Times* editorialized September 4, "At the heart of the Maoist thesis is the claim that the United States, and by implication any or all of the large industrial nations, can be defeated militarily by peasant masses organized for guerrilla combat."

century. They reached a precarious stalemate in Laos and put a parenthesis around Cambodia. Through their surrogate forces, the Viet Cong, they are making an all-out try to win a vintage-type "war of national liberation" in South Viet Nam. It is for this reason that Defense Secretary McNamara correctly predicted to the House Armed Forces Committee in February 1965 that the crucial test in this struggle to change the world balance of power would lie within the area of Southeast Asia.

In Thailand the Communists have made little headway, and the Thais have contributed significantly to the infrastructure of the war in Viet Nam. Burma hopes it has made its peace with Peking but follows a policy of steadfast neutrality. However, there are insurgent elements in Burma which could lend themselves nicely to the formula of a "war of national liberation." Further south lies Malaysia, threatened by an Indonesia where "anti-imperialist" nationalism reached hydrophobic proportions and Communists of the Chinese persuasion once waited hopefully for a ripe fruit to fall from the tree. Here, incidentally, the Soviets have made a dubious billion-dollar investment in military aid, much of it naval in character. Here also is a nation strung along 3500 miles of self-proclaimed *mare clausum* which is perhaps more vulnerable than any country on earth to the pressures of naval power.

Of all the potential areas for "wars of national liberation" only the small Himalayan states or entities are relatively immune from the reach of sea power (although not beyond the range of the attack carriers and the Polaris submarines). Kashmir is a candidate country, as well indicated by the recent rapprochement between Rawalpindi and Peking — to say nothing of the Chinese strategic road from Sinkiang through the Aksai Chin near Ladakh, whose route we have already traveled. Others include the Kingdom of Nepal, the princely states of Bhutan and Sikkim, and the North East Frontier Agency, threatened by Chinese armed attack in 1962. And there is Tibet, taken by armed force by Communist China in 1950, where anti-Communist guerrilla forces are biding their time to stage a "war of national liberation" in reverse.

Once again we return to sea power in contemplating the candidate countries of the Arab East and North Africa. In the Arab lands "Nasserite Socialism" may in fact forestall the Communist enemy by drawing off the steam of nationalism into its own vessels and by leading a crusade of "anti-imperialism" of its own. In fact, Communist parties are officially proscribed in each of the thirteen countries of the Arab League. However, no geographer of the areas of "national liberation" could fail to gazette such candidate possibilities as Yemen, where a civil war with outside intervention has recently been curbed; or the shaky South Arabian Federation whose Chief Minister at Aden in 1965 called for the fulfillment of a United Nations General Assembly resolution demanding withdrawal of the British base. The list might also include the Sheikdoms of the Trucial Coast and the Persian Gulf, protected by the Perpetual Peace; and such turbulent lands as Iraq and Syria. In Iraq the Kurdish war for autonomy if not independence has become perennial. The Arabian monarchies offer temptation for those who would overthrow the existing order, and questions of the succession of kings will arise in Saudi Arabia, Jordan, Libya and Morocco.

All of sub-Saharan Africa is an area of potential "national liberation" war. The countries are too numerous for this listing, but the interest of the Communist predators has been made manifest in the Soviet and later Chinese involvement in the Congo and repeated flights to Africa of that professional bird of ill omen, Chou En-lai.

However, all of Africa can be made subservient to sea power.

Another area of the earth which was discovered by sea, developed by sea and defended by sea is the Western Hemisphere. Here, in the American *mare nostrum*, the Caribbean, one important country, Cuba, has already been taken by Communist subversion. The Dominican Republic was a recent candidate; and Haiti, whose flag was made when the black insurgents tore the white center from the French Tricolor, is an obvious potential one. Across the Caribbean lie former British Guiana, one of the newest of the Commonwealth nations, whose recent Prime Minister is at least a crypto-Communist; and Venezuela, where in 1963 a major Communist coup was launched and failed. Also touching upon the neuralgic sea of the Antilles is Colombia, where more than a decade of senseless slaughter has decimated whole areas and the leadership of the now-diminishing bandit forces seems increasingly under Communist direction. North of the Isthmus and also touching upon the Caribbean are such countries as Guatemala, which not so many years ago had a quasi-Communist government, and such uneasy republics as Nicaragua and Honduras. Even in Panama, where U.S. influence has been continuous from the creation of the state, ugly outbreaks have shown the telltale stigmata of Communist-inspired riots, if not "wars" of "national liberation." So much for the untranquil Caribbean.

On the South American continent Bolivia is almost constantly on the boil. Ecuador and Paraguay are two other largely Indian nations which offer some of the conditions propitious to "wars of national liberation," but their present regimes are clearly alert to the fact.

One talks of revolutions elsewhere in South America, and in truth there have been many over the past score of years, but they seem not to relate to the phenomenon Vice President

Humphrey had in mind; and the recent return to constitutional order in Brazil and Guatemala, the dramatic defeat of
the Communists in the 1964 Chilean presidential election,
the orderly elections in the Dominican Republic in 1966 —
all give cause for optimism on the part of the Free World.

If, as has been said, "geography is the stage upon which
history is enacted," this is the chart of the candidate countries, the profile of the "soft under-belly of the world," the
atlas for anarchy which the Communists must study if they
plan a twenty-year strategy for "wars of national liberation."
The significant thing is the fact that of the sixty-eight candidate countries all, except six insignificant Himalayan entities on the Roof of the World between India and China, are
within the reach and the grasp of sea power.

4.

This is not to say, however, that the application of sea
power is the simple answer to the "war of national liberation," that "bold new form of aggression" which Vice President Humphrey says "could rank in military importance with
the discovery of gun powder." "Wars of national liberation"
have their military aspect, and the application of sea power
to that aspect will be discussed in due course; but at the outset it must be emphasized that the essence of this new type of
war is political. The Communist purpose is political, the
conditions precedent are political, the tactics are political,
and military means are used for political ends.

The United States, whose President and Secretaries of
State and Defense have acted on an instinct of history far
more acute than some journalists would have the world sup-
pose, was quick to analyze the nature of the Communist
threat and to adopt those measures of a political and economic nature which best suited the situation. In fact, the
whole new concept of foreign aid, as expressed in the Tru-

man Doctrine, the Marshall Plan, Point Four, the successive
Mutual Security Acts and the Alliance for Progress, was so
successful that our Communist adversaries, both the U.S.S.R.
and China, were forced to adopt similar programs. How
Lenin's Marxist dialectic would have explained this frank
plagiarism from the capitalist book has not been revealed.

Early in President Kennedy's administration, after the
fiasco of the Bay of Pigs, the crisis in the Congo and the continuance of the descending spiral in Southeast Asia, two new
defense-attack concepts were developed. One was military
— the Special Forces. The other was political and psychological — a brilliant concept with a bad name: Counter Insurgency.

The Army Special Forces, with their training center and
schools at Fort Bragg, present an intelligent and flexible approach to the military problem of guerrilla war. In essence
the Special Forces out-guerrilla the guerrillas. With their
superior communications and mobility, backed by air and
sea power, these troops above all profit from élan and esprit
de corps. It is regrettable that because they are unorthodox
the Special Forces do not fit into the T.O.'s and E.'s of the
more conventional commanders. Yet something of the nature of the Special Forces will be essential if the terrible
arithmetic of guerrilla war is to be made the algebra of a
more balanced equation.

Counter Insurgency, under the immediate personal eye of
President Kennedy and his brother, the Attorney General,
became a compulsory course for senior officials of the Foreign Service, the Armed Forces, Foreign Aid and personnel
of USIA and CIA. It involves detailed study of the Communist techniques of subversion and guerrilla war. The continuance of such study is essential to U.S. success in over-
coming the political-military invention of "wars of national
liberation."

However, the stress on counterinsurgency risks a static

attitude of mind, a predisposition for the status quo, a resistance to change which ill becomes the great Republic
founded upon revolution. There will be revolutions in the
world based on valid pressures for social and economic reform which may have nothing to do with Communism. Furthermore, we should be chary of building ourselves a new
trip-wire whereby any self-proclaimed coup "against Communism" automatically brings in the United States on the
side of repression. By preaching the negative theme of
Counter Insurgency the United States risks putting itself before the world as a sort of twentieth-century Metternich,
seeking to restore the past and to shore up a Holy Roman
Empire which, as Voltaire observed, was neither Empire,
Roman, nor Holy.

Instead, while continuing to study the techniques of subversion as expressed in "wars of national liberation," the
United States should adopt a more positive stance. As inheritors of the American Revolution and expositors of the
inalienable Rights of Man, we could do well to read out in
louder voice the Declaration of Independence. In fact we
might well call our worldwide effort to victory over these
sham "wars of national liberation" wars for freedom, or wars
for independence. Counter Insurgency is not the positive
call to affirmative action.

5.

What, then, should be the elements for a successful American strategy to win wars of independence against "wars of
national liberation"?

In this worldwide struggle all the elements of national
power must be deployed. The threat must be met in political
terms, in its social expression, by the precise use of our immense economic and financial strength, and by the imagina-

tive deployment of our armed forces. We should also not forget that our allies have obligations; and that one of the characteristics of limited war in the last half of the twentieth century is the use of surrogate forces.

A basic political prerequisite in fighting "wars of national liberation" is a clear understanding that "the Lord helps those who help themselves." There is no use in the United States' rushing in to save people who lack the will to save themselves. Nor are we the crew of a universal and automatic fire engine, dashing to put out every blaze ignited by small boys. But where people do want to live in peace and security and find their independence threatened and are willing to defend themselves, there is much we can do to help them to win.

The problem of motivation is basic to the winning or losing of "wars of national liberation." Military men take this as axiomatic, but the politicians must see it also. One of the reasons that French had to do the fighting in Indochina was the fact that few of the inhabitants of the Associated States really believed that France had any intention of setting them free. And no Vietnamese was willing to fight and die for Bao Dai, a puppet Chief of State so professional that he had served French and Japanese and Ho Chi Minh.

So although limited wars may be fought by surrogate forces, winning governments cannot be headed by foreign-installed puppets. Here the Communists run a risk inherently greater than our own. They seek under a false cliché to incite wars whose real purpose is not "national liberation" but international enslavement by Communist conspiracy, and they must of necessity find renegades to rule.

It goes without saying that in the political field, as in the military, personnel must be carefully trained for the job. Here the United States is doing well. In the early days of the old Diplomatic Service the only injunction was to "wear a clean shirt and sit with your back to the light." Even past World War II there was little emphasis on language training other than for the Japan and China hands, and for the slender cadre of Oriental Interpreters. Now the Foreign Service Institute, taking a leaf from the book of the Army and Navy language schools, gives instruction in practically all foreign languages. The writer recently talked with a dozen young Foreign Service Officers in training at Fort Bragg who were going out to South Viet Nam as provincial political officers. They brought their own Vietnamese language teacher with them to North Carolina so as not to miss a day's lesson.

Analogous to the use of trained Foreign Service and AID personnel in political and economic fields is the work of the Peace Corps, one of the genuinely new and unqualifiedly successful inventions of the Kennedy regime. The real goal of the Communist aim in "wars of national liberation" is the youth of the underdeveloped countries. If through our Peace Corps youngsters we can get to youth ahead of the Communists the game will be won for the Free World.

Cultural diplomacy, and especially the exchange of persons under the Fulbright, Smith-Mundt and private programs such as the admirable youth exchanges of the American Friends Service Committee, all contribute to the success of war against "wars of national liberation." The vast educational resources of the United States and other Free World countries are of vital importance in the struggle. The relative tranquillity of formerly French and British Africa owes much to the educational systems of France and the United Kingdom. In the Arab world the existence of the American University of Beirut is worth all our aid programs combined for those countries. In the countries candidate for "wars of national liberation" ignorance is one of the prime factors favoring the Communist side. Education dispels ignorance, and "the Truth shall set men free."

So much has been said about foreign aid programs that it may now be taken as axiomatic that aid will be used as an instrument of policy by both sides in fighting "wars of national liberation." We must be careful, however, not to put the European template of the Marshall Plan on underdeveloped countries where conditions are different and nationalism is an emotion as well as an ideal.

Thought should be given to the political advantage of land reform in fighting "wars of national liberation." We have taken land reform as one of the twelve objectives of the Alliance for Progress and much lip service is paid to it. Furthermore, under the MacArthur Shogunate the Americans imposed a singularly successful program of land reform in Japan. However, in South Viet Nam, where the Viet Cong freely promise what is not theirs to give — land for all the peasants — we have done practically nothing to counter this significant appeal. Even if we should have to pay for expropriated landlords' property in order to give land to the peasants on our side, the price would be little in comparison with the military costs of war. We should in addition exploit the evident fact that agriculture under Communism has been a dismal failure, both in the Soviet Union and in mainland China.

6.

These considerations on the surface may seem remote from military power. But "wars of national liberation" are a new concept which has to be dealt with by imaginative new means, including military power. Bernard B. Fall, the historian of the wars in Viet Nam, has defined "revolutionary war" in the wars in Viet Nam, by the formula $RW = P + GW$: revolutionary war equals political activity plus guerrilla war. Yet the intelligent application of force, and in particular sea power, may yet spell defeat to the Communist cause.

With the exception of South and Southeast Asia, geography is against the Communists, and even here sea power of the West is supreme in the Western Pacific, the China Seas and the Indian Ocean. Looking outward from Moscow or Peking, the strategists of "wars of national liberation" face a dismal logistical prospect. The admiral in charge of the Far East Fleet at Vladivostok must scratch his head as to how to help such a pelagic state as Indonesia. Despite the repeated visits of Chou En-lai to both coasts of Africa and the Mediterranean littoral, how does Chinese economic and military strength become manifest on that continent except by sea? In the Americas, the naval quarantine of Cuba, backed up by overwhelming air and terrestrial forces, compelled Khrushchev to put his rockets in reverse.

So, although the twenty-second Communist Congress might vote a resolution calling for a twenty-year strategy of "wars of national liberation," it could not, any more than King Canute, forbid the moving of the tide. And the tide is with us. It is the tide of sea power.

The numbered Fleets have placed a parenthesis about the potential thrust of Communism. The Sixth and Seventh Fleets provide the most mobile and modulated means of response to Communist attempts at subversive war west, south and east of the Communist land mass, while able allies, including the British at Singapore and the Australians with their new defense complex in Queensland, help close the gap in the Indian Ocean and South China Sea. Here, incidentally and eventually perhaps significantly, one should take note of the remarkable letter addressed to the *New York Times* on May 27, 1965, by the former Governor General of India, C. Rajagopalachari, in which he proposed a tripartite alliance of the United States, India and Japan, on the grounds that "there is no hope to get out of this great tangle unless India and Japan realize their duty in this connection and enter into a firm solemn defense treaty for defending the free way of life against the advance of Communism, and act swiftly."

In the Western Hemisphere no country, including the dynamite-swinging tin miners of Juan Lechin in Bolivia, is immune from the reach of sea power. Here the long and constructive history of Operation Unitas, the annual, multinational exercise of fleets of the United States and the South American Republics, provides a pattern as to how sea power can be made effective against those who would start "wars of national liberation."

In the Antilles, Cuba and the Dominican Republic have dramatized the use of sea power in the containment and curtailment of Communism. In the Western Pacific, sea power brought the troops to Korea, maintained the Okinawa bastion, defended Taiwan and the Philippines, and is currently deployed on the coast of Viet Nam. The entire line of communications of Free World forces in East Asia depends on sea power. The economic aid programs could not be made manifest without control of the sea. And naval blockade could stifle the export of anthracite from Haiphong, the import of needed supplies to Hanoi.

In the extraordinarily complex and delicate operations required to redress Dr. Fall's equation for "revolutionary war," sea power provides the most complete and subtle mix of forces. Naval air power ranges from the variety of weapons and vehicles afforded by the attack carriers to the defensive complex of the anti-submarine groups to the vertical envelopment capability of the helicopter carriers and the Marines. The amphibious warfare forces can land practically anywhere the oceans of the world lap a beach. Under the sea submarines can protect friendly forces or interdict unfriendly shipping. Mastery of the sea permits the bringing into the right spot at the right time both tonnage of goods and multiples of manpower. Furthermore, under good old Grotius' law, access to within three miles of any coast is unlimited; the Navy does not have to ask passage rights for the untrammeled reaches of the sea. *

So in summary it would seem that those who would upset the balance of world power within the framework of the atomic deterrent may find that sea power will prove the ultimate stumbling block. Those areas of the world presumably ripe for Communist subversion are encompassed by ocean. Thus far in history, with the exception of Cuba, there has been no Communist takeover of a country without the presence or proximity of massive Communist land forces. And although the primary area of struggle will be political and economic, and the essential conflict will be within men's minds, the element of military power will not be lacking, and military power cannot be brought to bear throughout most of the undeveloped world by those who do not control the sea.

If, in fact, the invention of "wars of national liberation" may rank in military importance with the invention of gunpowder, there is reason to be the more alert but no reason to be less confident of victory. Some people, fooling with gunpowder, have been hoist with their own petard. The challenge primarily is one for our diplomacy; but effective diplomacy has always been linked with military power. In the opening situations sea power may provide the affirmative answer. When the new crises beset us, let us remember that with danger comes opportunity.

---

* In thus laying emphasis on sea power, the author does not at all wish to underestimate the attributes of land and air power. He was too much a witness of the effectiveness of these arms in Lebanon to ignore their contribution in the joint peace-keeping task served by all elements of the Defense Department.

CHAPTER XII

The Lessons of Limited War

1.

IN 1960 a Norwegian statistician asked a computer how many wars there had been in 5560 years of recorded human history. The machine produced the statistic that there had been 14,-531 wars in that space of time or 2.6135 a year. In fact only ten years of all of human history had been years of uninterrupted peace.[1] War, therefore, seems to be a condition of man's self-made environment, but as we have seen, in the latter half of the twentieth century, with the atomic balance of power and in the era of the *pax ballistica,* war is limited in scope, objective and character.

We have in this book studied all except one of the seven categories of limited war by the case method. We have studied limited strategic war in Greece and Korea; war for independence in the case of Israel; a war for limited political and strategic objectives, of which the example was Suez; civil war with outside intervention, as in Lebanon; war for the acquisition of territory, as in the Chinese attack on the Himalayan frontier of India; and "wars of national liberation," of which the archetype is Viet Nam. Only that form of limited war which is domestic rebellion without outside intervention has not formed a part of our case study.

One authority has listed thirty, another forty, limited wars which have been fought since 1945. Each of these falls within the categories outlined above. According to this latter study, twenty-three of the forty wars involved Communist participation. Of the remaining seventeen conflicts, eight were anti-colonial struggles ranging from the Indonesian rebellion against the Netherlands through the Kenya Mau-Mau "emergency" to the struggle for independence in Algeria. Another six of the limited wars fought since 1945 fall into the category of neighbor against neighbor, such as the Pakistani-Indian war in 1947–1949 and its recent recurrence in 1965.[2]

It is therefore possible from this wealth of historic evidence to draw conclusions as to the nature of limited war in the last half of the twentieth century. Although, as has been pointed out, in the *pax ballistica* unlimited weapons limit themselves, some limited wars have had seemingly limitless consequences. We have seen the chain of circumstance which began with Stalin's intervention in Greece which gave rise to the Truman Doctrine, the Marshall Plan, and NATO. Similarly, on the other side of the world, Stalin's intervention in Korea achieved for the West the gigantic strategic consequence of defeating a Communist thrust for dominance in the Western Pacific. Of equally enormous strategic importance was the French war in Viet Nam and its sequel, the American struggle to prevent the neuralgic peninsula of Southeast Asia from falling into Communist hands and thus severing the connection between the Indian and Pacific oceans.

However, although limited wars may have limitless consequences they all have the characteristics of limitations as to the theater of war, the forces concerned, and the objectives of the war; and it must ever be kept in mind that the objectives of limited war are political. Our adversaries have clearly recognized this fact as the writings of Lenin and Mao Tse-tung eloquently prove. The current doctrines which

animate Communist China postulate the political character
of war as fundamental to any understanding of it. Mao Tse-
tung in his book *On the Protracted War* is replete in his itera-
tion and reiteration of the same point: "War is politics, war
itself is a political action; war cannot for a single moment be
separated from politics; any tendency . . . to belittle politics, to isolate war from politics, and to become advocates of
'war is everything' is erroneous and must be corrected." [3]

And as Général d'Armée André Beaufre, perhaps France's
leading expert on strategy, has stated, "limited wars are a
sort of tough negotiation; and therefore they should not be
won on the spot . . . limited wars are not intended to win,
but not to be defeated. *The essential is to be still there.*" [4]

From the evidence studied it is apparent that there are
several almost unique characteristics of late-twentieth-cen-
tury limited war. These include the use of surrogate forces;
respect for sanctuary; and the new Communist political invention of "wars of national liberation."

2.

The use of someone else's soldiers to do your fighting is not
unique in history. Ever since the time of Xenophon and the
Ten Thousand to the British use of the Indian Army in two
world wars and their continuing utilization of Nepalese
Gurka troops, the surrogate soldier has had his place in history. However, it does seem a characteristic of limited war in
the twentieth century that the use of surrogate forces is in
some cases predominant. The wars in Greece, Korea, and
Viet Nam make the point.

The corollary to the use of surrogate forces has been massive support from outside the belligerent area or state furnished by interested powers. The degree of such aid varies
from the truly extraordinary proportions of the Vietnamese

war to the relatively modest outside intervention in the civil war in Lebanon. Yet in most cases of limited war in this century it is as true today as when Thucydides wrote that "it is not in Attica that the war will be decided . . . but in the countries by which Attica is supported." [5]

Respect for sanctuary has been carried to an extraordinary extent in twentieth-century limited war. We have seen in the case of Greece that it was not until Tito was excommunicated by Stalin that the sanctuary in Thrace and Macedonia was denied the Communist guerrillas. Korea provided a more dramatic example of sanctuary, with unlimited aid being supplied to one side by the Communists from Manchuria and Siberia and to the other by the United States from the insular sanctuary of Japan. In this most rigorously limited of limited wars, the American Air Force was forbidden to bomb beyond the Yalu or even to chase MIGs which returned to the sanctuary. However, on the other side the MIGs did not seek to bomb the numerous U.S. bases in South Korea or in Japan; and both sides respected the sanctuary of the sea. In the Lebanese civil war Syria afforded sanctuary to the Moslem insurgents; while in the Vietnamese wars there was the immense sanctuary of South China and respect for sanctuaries at sea on both sides. It was not until the episode at the Tonkin Gulf and the attack at Pleiku in 1965 that the United States decided to disregard to some extent the sanctity of sanctuary; but even here the targets were rigorously limited to military objectives and were so tightly scheduled that no bombs fell without the express permission of the White House. This indeed was a limitation in limited war.

A chapter has been devoted to that special characteristic of twentieth-century limited war, the Communist "wars of national liberation." However, it is much to be doubted if Mao's insistence that "the countryside and the countryside alone can provide the revolutionary bases from which the revolutionaries can go forward to final victory" [6] is in accord with historical fact. On the contrary, it would seem that Lenin made a more lucid analysis in postulating that the ultimate victory of the revolutionary proletariat would come in two stages and be preceded by a bourgeois revolution.

As for the ultimate outcome of this Communist attempt to change the world balance of power by subversive political war, it would seem that there are more assets on the side of the West than on the side of Red revolution. The countries which are candidates for "wars of national liberation" can be saved from this threat by sea power.

3.

Another characteristic of twentieth-century limited war is the fact that international organization has played an important role, either in settling these armed conflicts or as serving as a useful palliative and sally port for belligerents in need of saving face. Other limited wars in history have, of course, been brought to diplomatic solutions through the Concert of Powers; but international organization itself, and here we speak largely of the United Nations, had not reached that point of evolution where it could play a useful role.

Of the wars studied in this book, the United Nations took action in the cases of Greece, Korea, Palestine, Suez, Lebanon, and to a certain extent, in Indochina in sending a commission of investigation to Cambodia. The Security Council was seized of the war in Viet Nam on January 31, 1966 but thus far has done little about it. The United Nations also took cognizance of and had a role in limited wars which have not formed the object of this study. These include the war for Indonesian independence, the Kashmir dispute between Pakistan and India, the Hungarian rebellion, the civil war in Cyprus, and the civil war in the Congo; the question of "West

Irian" between the Netherlands and Indonesia, the U.S. landing in the Dominican Republic in 1965 and ultimately the brief Indo-Pakistan war of the same year.

However, there have been numerous other limited wars without United Nations intervention. These would include the Communist Hukbalahap insurrection in the Philippines; the French phase of the Indochinese war; the guerrilla war in Malaya; the Mau Mau "episode" in Kenya; the Chinese occupation of Tibet in 1950 and the Tibetan rebellion in 1959; the Quemoy-Matsu crisis of 1958; the Sino-Indian conflict on the Himalayan frontier in 1962; the Algerian rebellion; the Laotian civil war; the British intervention at Kuwait in response to an Iraqi threat; the Indian occupation of Goa; the civil war in Yemen with outside intervention by the U.A.R. and Saudi Arabia; and the ever-smoldering struggle of the Kurds for independence from Iraq.

The United Nations has been most effective when the two super-powers have voted the same ticket. This was illustrated in the cases of Palestine, Suez, and the Indo-Pakistan limited war of 1965. The U.N. has likewise been effective when the U.S.S.R. has been absent from the Security Council, as in the case of Korea, or has been outvoted by the General Assembly, as in the cases of Greece and the civil war in the Congo. However, the U.N. has been ineffective in the cases where the Communist powers have operated from contiguous territories, as in the case of Hungary and that of Tibet. The U.N. has also not been effective when other regional organizations, e.g. the OAS in the Dominican Republic case, have already been seized of the problem. This, technically speaking, is, however, foreseen and provided for in Chapter VIII of the Charter.

On the whole, U.N. concern with the settlement of limited wars has been salutary. The diplomacy of Dag Hammarskjöld and Lester Pearson in 1956, using the United Nations as a major instrument for peace-making in extricating France, the United Kingdom and Israel from the consequences of their adventure at Suez, is a dramatic case in point. Similarly. it cannot be doubted that the U.N. peace-keeping forces in Palestine, the Gaza Strip, and in Cyprus have been of great utility in maintaining uneasy armistices in the Eastern Mediterranean.

4.

The conduct of limited war has resulted in the evolution of a sort of pragmatic philosophy as to how they should be conducted. *The Economist* summed it up most succinctly in the statement quoted in the preface to this work: "The first of the rules of confrontation is that one should make one's objectives clear, and the second that one should do the least that is necessary to achieve them." The quiet understatement of General Beaufre that "limited wars are a sort of tough negotiation," should be contrasted with the bombast of General MacArthur, who while he admitted never having studied the question of limited war, shouted that "there is no substitute for victory." In this he appealed to the ingrained American emotion that war somehow or other is like an athletic contest in which ties are rare and victory or defeat is the only outcome. What the American people are slowly learning is a question of endurance and discipline and patience with great objectives to be won which are indeed a valid "substitute for victory."

At the same time we must give heed to President Eisenhower's caution of finding ourselves victims of the tyrannies of the weak. As the General wrote his friend Swede Hazlett: "In the effort to promote the rights of all, and observe the equality of sovereignty as between the great and small, we unavoidably give to the little nations opportunities to embarrass us greatly." [7]

As *The Economist* said, the first of the rules of confrontation is that one should make one's objectives clear. Here we come to the requirement of limited war for precise "communication." It is essential in this form of political-military exercise that there be correct evaluation of the other side's objectives, motives, limitations, and above all, psychology. This is of inordinate importance in dealing with the Communists, who view the world through the distorting spectacles of Marx, Lenin, and Mao Tse-tung. In fact, the greatest danger in dealing with Peking is the mal-focus and limitation of information which reaches the men who make the decisions. If all the Chinese Government has to go on are the writings of Mao Tse-tung and the metaphysics of Marshal Lin Piao, supplemented by daily readings from Hsin Hua, the official Communist News Agency, it would be bold indeed to conclude that their estimate of the situation was either objective or unemotional. And for our part we must guard against the tendency to evaluate the motives and objectives of Asian peoples as we would our own.

Yet, despite these difficulties in communication and in the correct evaluation of motives, our study of limited war clearly indicates that there are markers given by both sides in a conflict which furnish clear indices of impending action. Thus, in the war in Korea there was a very explicit prior warning from Peking that if American troops crossed the 38th parallel Red Chinese troops would join battle. In the case of Nehru's protracted negotiation with Chou En-lai over the frontier dispute between India and China, the warnings of Peking grew ever more explicit and shrill but were disregarded by the Indian statesman. At the same time, in this vitally important process of evaluation and communication one must keep in mind what James Reston has called "Bohlen's law": "In dealing with the Communists, remember that in their mind what is secret is serious, and what is public is merely propaganda." [8]

5.

Another characteristic of limited war in the twentieth century is one derived not from limited war *per se* but from the fact of the atomic deterrent. This is the recent phenomenon of Task Force Commanders in limited war situations being the President of the United States or Chairman of the Soviet Presidium themselves. In the *pax ballistica* there has emerged a new dimension of risk — of what one authority has called the danger of "irreversibility becoming irremediable";[9] and thus we find an extraordinary new limitation on limited war — that the President himself or the Chairman of the Soviet Council of Ministers may make the smallest tactical decisions. The process commenced with President Truman in Korea and continued with the "eyeball-to-eyeball" confrontation of Kennedy and Khrushchev over Cuba, to the personal interventions of President Johnson as Task Force Commander in the Gulf of Tonkin and at the American landing in Santo Domingo. Where in past wars the military commander was given military objectives to achieve and told to go on with the task, in present limited war the military objectives must be so carefully evaluated by the Chief of Government to prevent escalation into general war, and the political objective must be so clearly kept in mind, that the military commander is now an executive agent at one or two removes from the real source of decision and power.

A Foreign Service colleague, Martin Herz, the distinguished author of the book, *The Origins of the Cold War*, has offered this further comment:

> One aspect of limited war that is entirely legitimate, even though it crowds the boundaries of your subject, is the *ability* to escalate. Intelligent participants in limited war will not do it, and the doctrine of limited war prohibits it, but since the borderline between limited war and general war is

not always easy to define, this shadow area might be a little more explored in your book. Limited war between two sides of which one is capable of escalating while the other is not, is surely different from limited war between two sides that are really in balance. I am not, please, advocating "brinkmanship," but there seems to me an important distinction between limited wars that involve the big powers, even if indirectly, and limited wars that do not or that involve them more remotely. That, incidentally, is why communication between the enemies about escalation is so important.

6

One byproduct of twentieth-century limited war is perhaps peculiar to the United States. This has been the development of the Country Team. We have seen how the early chaotic structure of the American operation in Greece, with two autonomous ambassadors and a variety of highly independent military chieftains, led to prompt recognition of the need to put the official American overseas house in order. The evolution of the Country Team became all the more mandatory with the proliferation of U.S. military groups or MAAGs throughout the world in the countries to which mutual assistance and military aid was furnished; and in an equal proliferation of economic aid missions and the propaganda apparatus of the United States Information Service.

To orchestrate the various activities of American officialdom abroad therefore became an urgent and imperative task. Although the first use of the term "Country Team" was made in a paper written by General Clay in 1951, it was not until November 6, 1954, in President Eisenhower's Executive Order of that date that in fact order was wrought out of a pre-existing chaos, and the American Ambassador in any given country was made *primus inter pares* among the various elements of the Country Team. The evolution of the legislative process in the functioning of the Country Team reached its final expression in the letter addressed to all American Ambassadors by President Kennedy on May 29, 1961:

> In regard to your personal authority and responsibility, I shall count on you to oversee and coordinate all the activities of the United States Government in _____.
>
> You are in charge of the entire U.S. Diplomatic Mission, and I shall expect you to supervise all of its operations. The Mission includes not only the personnel of the Department of State and the Foreign Service, but also the representatives of all other U.S. agencies which have programs or activities in _____.
>
> As you know, the U.S. Diplomatic Mission includes service attachés, military assistance advisory groups, and other military components attached to the Mission. It does not, however, include U.S. military forces operating in the field where such forces are under the command of a U.S. area military commander. The line of authority to these forces runs from me, to the Secretary of Defense, to the Joint Chiefs of Staff in Washington and to the area commander in the field.
>
> Although this means that the Chief of the American Diplomatic Mission is not in the line of military command, nevertheless, as Chief of Mission you should work closely with the appropriate area military commander to assure the full exchange of information. If it is your opinion that activities by the U.S. military forces may adversely affect our overall relations with the people or government of _____, you should promptly discuss the matter with the military commander and, if necessary, request a decision by higher authority.[10]

In a smoothly operating Country Team the Ambassador is the top man. He is not only the administrator of policy, but the coordinator of every effort of his large governmental staff, irrespective of what Department or Agency in Washington they work for. This imposes a formidable task on the Ambassador; but an able Chief of Mission who knows how to lead his colleagues will have no difficulty in establishing rapport with his staff, talking their own language, eliciting from them the information he needs on which to base his recommendations on policy, and in giving them in return the necessary guidance for the conduct in the field of their specialization of U.S. foreign policy in the country where they are stationed. Thus the ideal administration of a Country Team may be likened to the conduct of a symphony orchestra in which the Ambassador gets a harmonious response from its members in playing policy music for which the President has set the theme.

On March 4, 1966, President Johnson extended the Country Team principle to Washington. In the words of Secretary of State Rusk,

> The President has assigned to me and the Department of State additional responsibility for the over-all direction, coordination and supervision of the inter-departmentral activities of the United States Government overseas.
>
> This assignment extends to the limits permitted by law and covers all operations of the United States Government abroad except U.S. military forces under area military command and such other military activities as the President may elect to conduct through military channels.
>
> The President's directive also established a systematic mechanism for considering the views of other agencies involved in our activities abroad, and for reaching decisions promptly.
>
> This responsibility will be discharged in Washington primarily through the Under Secretary and the regional Assistant Secretaries of State. They will be assisted by interdepartmental groups of which they will be executive chair-

men with full powers of decision on all matters within their purview.

Thus, the Department, and the regional Assistant Secretaries with respect to their geographic areas, will exercise leadership functions and responsibilities at the seat of Government similar to those delineated for Ambassadors within the countries of their assignment by the President's action of May 1961.[11]

7.

Throughout this study the role of diplomacy has been implicit in any consideration of limited war. Limited wars are explicit instruments of foreign policy; they are therefore extensions by force of diplomacy. Without clear-cut political objectives limited wars become meaningless, and military victory an empty expression. This is the fallacy in the atomic age and the era of limited war of clinging to the MacArthur concept of there being "no substitute for victory." The substitute for victory in our age is lasting peace and the turning of men's aims and energies away from war. Otherwise, victory in the *pax ballistica* will fit the definition of the *Pax Romana* made twenty centuries ago by the Caledonian chief, Galgaeus: "They make a desert, and call it peace."

Perhaps we may be permitted to hope that once the terrible test of the Communist theory of "wars of national liberation" has been put to the proof and the theory proved false, as it will be, there will ensue an era of "peaceful coexistence" sustained by the atomic balance of power and kept in equilibrium by diplomacy.

There may even come that millennium described by Edgar Snow in his last interview with Mao Tse-tung — "Mao's voice dropped away, and he half closed his eyes. Man's condition on this earth was changing with ever increasing rapidity. 'A thousand years from now all of them,' he said, 'even Marx, Engels and Lenin, would possibly appear rather ridiculous.' " [12]

It is the thousand-year view that the statesman must assume, and in this perspective the diplomat may take hope from history. The twentieth century has demonstrated the terminal folly of general war, and the atomic Aladdin closely guards his genie in the lamp. Feats of arms there will continue to be, but gradually there will dawn the comprehension that feats of moral and mental prowess are of equal difficulty and more lasting validity. Therefore the diplomatist will seek unceasingly to put increasing limitations upon war until ultimately the conflicts of interest, pride and ambition can be settled at the conference table and by the might of right. Perhaps the end of this century will disclose that the most dangerous of all the animals, man, has learned to tame himself and that a new era of his redemption has opened. Then, having at last secured his home base, he can embark in outer space and find his future in the stars.

NOTES

INDEX

Notes

Preface

1. Seymour J. Deitchman: *Limited War and American Defense Policy*. The M.I.T. Press, Cambridge, Massachusetts, 1964.
2. Morton H. Halpern: "Limited War." An essay on the development of the theory and an annotated bibliography. Harvard Center for International Affairs No. 3, May 1962.

Chapter I
Limited War and the Development of U.S. Defense Policy

1. Karl von Clausewitz: *On War*. Translated from the German by Matthijs Jolles. Combat Forces Press, Washington, D.C., 1953, p. 16.
2. Washington Center on Foreign Policy Research, Johns Hopkins University: *U.S. Foreign Policy: Developments in Military Technology and Their Impact on U.S. Strategy and Foreign Policy*. December 6, 1939, p. 14.
3. Général d'Armée André Beaufre: *An Introduction to Strategy*. Praeger, New York–Washington, 1965, p. 85. Cf. also Roger Trinquier: *Modern Warfare*, Praeger, New York–London, 1961, pp. 6–9.
4. Maxwell D. Taylor: *The Uncertain Trumpet*. Harper, New York, 1959, p. 4.
5. *Bulletin of the Atomic Scientists*. July 1950, pp. 194ff.
6. Taylor, *op. cit.*, p. 6.
7. *Ibid.*, pp. 7–8.

Chapter III
The Civil War in Greece

1. Bickham Sweet-Escott: *Greece, A Political and Economic Survey, 1939-1953.* Royal Institute of International Affairs, London and New York, 1952, p. 32.
2. *Ibid.,* pp. 36-39.
3. Report by the Commission of Investigation Concerning Greek Frontier Incidents to the Security Council, S/360, May 27, 1947, 3 vols.
4. *Ibid.,* June 30, 1948, p. 61 n. 2.
5. Harry S Truman: *Memoirs,* Vol. II, *Years of Trial and Hope.* Doubleday, Garden City, N.Y., 1958, p. 99.
6. *Ibid.,* p. 99.
7. *Ibid.*
8. *Ibid.,* p. 100.
9. *Ibid.,* p. 106.
10. *Ibid.*
11. *Ibid.,* p. 107.
12. *Ibid.,* p. 108.
13. *Ibid.,* p. 99.
14. *Ibid.,* p. 109.

In 1962-63, the Department of State coordinated various interdepartmental studies of "counterinsurgency" as the result of President Kennedy's interest in exploring every facet of the defense policy of flexible response. One of these studies was entitled, "U.S. Military Participation in the Counter-Insurgency Operation in Greece, 1947-1949." Although as a draft interagency study this paper never assumed official status and was never approved, even by the interagency group charged with its preparation, it does cast useful side lights on the civil war in Greece. Henceforth cited as USMP-Greece.

15. USMP-Greece, p. 7. *See* note 14.
16. *Ibid.,* p. 8.
17. *Ibid.,* p. 10.
18. *Ibid.,* p. 13.
19. *Ibid.,* p. 19.
20. *Ibid.,* p. 15.

21. *Ibid.*, p. 102.
22. *Ibid.*, p. 137.
23. *Ibid.*, pp. 109–110.
24. *Ibid.*, p. 112.
25. Sweet-Escott, *op. cit.*, p. 60.
26. USMP–Greece, *op. cit.*, p. 20.
27. Council of Ministers Decision No. 62 and 63, January 20, 1949, cited in USMP–Greece, *op. cit.*, p. 123.
28. Kingdom of Greece, Emergency Law 882, Art. 2, January 20, 1949, cited in USMP–Greece, *op. cit.*, p. 124.
29. Sweet-Escott, *op. cit.*, p. 41.
30. G.H.N. Seton-Watson: "Yugoslavia," *Encyclopedia Britannica*, 1962, Vol. 23.
31. Sweet-Escott, *op. cit.*, p. 63.
32. *Ibid.*
33. *Ibid.*, p. 62.
34. *Ibid.*
35. *Ibid.*, p. 70.
36. Geoffrey Chandler: *The Divided Land.* Macmillan, London, 1959, pp. 195–196.
37. Sweet-Escott, *op. cit.*, p. 70.
38. UNSCOB Fourth Report, para. 126.
39. Chandler, *op. cit.*, p. 202.
40. USMP–Greece, *op. cit.*, pp. 31–37.
41. Sweet-Escott, *op. cit.*, p. 63.

(Cf. also Twentieth Century Fund: *Report on the Greeks.* York, 1948, and F. A. Voight, *The Greek Sedition*, Hollis and Carter, London, 1949.)

Chapter IV
The War in Korea, 1950–1953

1. G. B. Sansom: *Japan, A Short Cultural History*, Revised Edition, Appleton-Century-Crofts, New York, 1962, pp. 410–413.
   Homer B. Hulbert: *The Passing of Korea.* Doubleday, Page and Co., New York, 1906, pp. 95, 98, 101.
2. Arthur L. Grey, Jr.: "The Thirty-Eighth Parallel," *Foreign Affairs*, Vol. 29, No. 3, April 1951, p. 485.

3. *Foreign Relations of the United States: Diplomatic Papers: The Conferences at Malta and Yalta 1945.* U.S. Government Printing Office, Washington, 1955, pp. 894–897.
4. Robert Leckie: *Conflict — The History of the Korean War, 1950–1953.* Putnam's, New York, 1962, p. 31.
5. *Ibid.,* pp. 29, 32.
6. Report of Government Section Supreme Allied Commander for the Allied Powers: *Political Reorientation of Japan September 1945 to September 1948.* U.S. Government Printing Office, Washington, no date; Appendices, p. 442.
7. Leckie, *op. cit.,* p. 24.
8. *Ibid.,* p. 35.
9. Department of State: *North Korea: A Case Study in the Techniques of Takeover.* Department of State Publication 7118, Far Eastern Series 103, released January 1961. U.S. Government Printing Office, Washington, p. 3.
   See also:
   Leckie, *op. cit.,* p. 26.
   Max Beloff: *Soviet Policy in the Far East, 1944–1951.* Oxford University Press, London, 1953, pp. 169–183.
10. Leckie, *op. cit.,* p. 35.
11. *Ibid.,* pp. 38–39.
12. *Ibid.,* p. 162.
    Harry S Truman: *Memoirs:* Vol. II, *Years of Trial and Hope.* Doubleday, Garden City, N.Y., 1956, p. 362.
    K. M. Panikkar: *In Two Chinas.* Allen and Unwin, London, 1955, p. 110.
13. Leckie, *op. cit.,* pp. 161–62. 169.
    Whiting, Allen S.: *China Crosses the Yalu, The Decision to Enter the Korean War.* The MacMillan Co., New York, 1960, pp. 143, 145.
14. Leckie, *op. cit.,* p. 165.
15. Leckie, *op. cit.,* pp. 171, 179, 180, 181.
16. Whiting, *op. cit.,* p. 118.
17. *Ibid.,* pp. 40–45, 152–159, 160.
18. Truman, *op. cit.,* p. 362.
19. *Ibid.,* pp. 406–407.
20. U.S. Senate: *Hearings Before the Committee on Armed*

Services and the Committee on Foreign Relations [the "MacArthur Hearings"] Eighty-second Congress, First Session, 5 Vols., U.S. Government Printing Office, Washington, 1951, I, pp. 324; II, pp. 730–733, 1188, 1385.

21. *Ibid.*, I, pp. 11–14, 81–84, 101–104, 221.
    Leckie, *op. cit.*, p. 268.
22. Truman, *op. cit.*, p. 450.
23. Senate Hearings, *op. cit.*, I, pp. 39–40.
24. Leckie, *op. cit.*, pp. 294–295.
25. *Ibid.*, pp. 299–315.
26. Dwight D. Eisenhower: *The White House Years: Mandate for Change, 1953–1957*. Doubleday, Garden City, N.Y., 1963, Vol. I, p. 171.
27. *Ibid.*, p. 95.
28. *Ibid.*, p. 123.
29. *Ibid.*, pp. 180–181.
    See also:
    John Robinson Beal: *John Foster Dulles, A Biography*. Harper, New York, 1957.
    Roscoe Drummond and Gaston Coblentz: *Duel at the Brink, John Foster Dulles, Command of American Power*, Doubleday and Co., Garden City, N.Y., 1960.
    Rutherford Poats: *Decision in Korea*, McBride, New York, 1954, p. 255.
30. Leckie, *op. cit.*, pp. 372–374.
31. Christoper Norred, Korean Desk Officer, Department of State. *See also* Poats, *op. cit.*, p. 255ff.
32. Leckie, *op. cit.*, pp. 375–384.
33. Panikkar, *op. cit.*, p. 108.
34. Leckie, *op. cit.*, p. 387.

Chapter V
Limited War for National Independence:
The Israeli-Arab War, 1947–1949

1. Polk, Stamlos and Asfour: *Backdrop to Tragedy:* The Struggle for Palestine. Beacon Press, Boston, 1957, p. 58. Henceforth cited as Polk, etc.

2. Polk, etc., *op. cit.*, p. 61.
3. *Ibid.*, p. 61.
4. *Ibid.*, p. 64.
5. *Foreign Relations of the United States 1943*. Vol. IV, pp. 786–787.
6. Polk, etc., *op. cit.*, p. 185.
7. *Ibid.*, p. 184.
8. Harry S Truman: *Memoirs*, Vol. II, *Years of Trial and Hope*. Doubleday, Garden City, N.Y., 1956, p. 133.
   See also Robert E. Sherwood: *Roosevelt and Hopkins, An Intimate History*. Harper, New York, 1948, pp. 871–872.
9. Jon and David Kimche: *Both Sides of the Hill: Britain and the Palestine War*. Secker and Warburg, London, 1960, pp. 45–46.
   Truman, *op. cit.*, p. 149.
10. Sir John Bagot Glubb: *A Soldier with the Arabs*. Harper, New York, 1957, p. 58.
11. Kimche, *op. cit.*, pp. 47, 50, 51.
12. Glubb, *op. cit.*, p. 45.
13. Quoted in The Political History of Palestine Under British Administration (Memo for UNSCOP), Jerusalem, 1947.
14. Kimche, *op. cit.*, pp. 55, 56, 57, 60, 79.
15. *Ibid.*, p. 60.
16. Glubb, *op. cit.*, pp. 63–66.
17. Kimche, *op. cit.*, pp. 66, 76.
18. Truman, *op. cit.*, p. 158.
19. Glubb, *op. cit.*, p. 79.
20. *Ibid.*, p. 81.
21. Kimche, *op. cit.*, p. 162.
22. Glubb, *op. cit.*, p. 94.
23. Truman, *op. cit.*, p. 164.
24. Kimche, *op. cit.*, p. 248.
25. Kimche, *op. cit.*, pp. 243–253, 256, 260–262.
    For a description of the U.N. Truce and mediation machinery, see David Brook: *Preface to Peace;* The United Nations and the Arab-Israel Armistice System. Public Affairs Press, Washington, 1964.
26. Kimche, *op. cit.*, pp. 266–271.

B. Walter Eyten: *The First Ten Years:* A Diplomatic History of Israel. Simon and Schuster, New York, 1958, pp. 28–48.
Glubb, *op. cit.*, pp. 233–237.

27. Musa Alami: *Ibrat Falastin.* Beirut, 1949. Condensed as "The Lesson of Palestine" in *Middle East Journal,* October 1949, Vol. 3, No. 4, Washington, pp. 373–405.
See also Constantine Zurayk: *Ma'na al Nakbah* (The Meaning of the Disaster). Kashaf Press, Beirut, 1948, 87 pp.
For a highly readable account of the military operations, see also Edgar O'Ballance, *The Arab-Israeli War 1948.* Praeger, New York, 1957, 220 pp.

Chapter VI
Sinai and Suez

1. Terence Robertson: *Crisis: The Inside Story of the Suez Conspiracy.* Atheneum, New York, 1965, p. 48.
1. *Ibid.*, p. 62.
3. Robert Murphy: *Diplomat Among Warriors.* Doubleday, Garden City, N.Y., 1964, p. 337.
Robertson, *op. cit.*, pp. 66–67.
4. *Ibid.*, p. 69.
5. *Ibid.*, p. 71.
A. J. Barker: *Suez: The Seven Day War.* Praeger, New York, 1964, p. 17.
6. Robertson, *op. cit.*, p. 71.
7. Murphy, *op. cit.*, p. 380.
8. Robertson, *op. cit.*, p. 22.
9. Henri Azeau: *Le Piege de Suez.* Robert Laffont, Paris, 1964, pp. 51–52.
10. *Ibid.*, p. 124.
11. Robertson, *op. cit.*, p. 48.
Azeau, *op. cit.*, pp. 102, 126.
12. Murphy, *op. cit.*, pp. 383–384.
Robertson, *op. cit.*, p. 78.
Dwight D. Eisenhower: *The White House Years: Waging Peace, 1956–1961.* Doubleday, Garden City, N.Y., 1965, chapters II and III, pp. 20–102.

13. Robertson, *op. cit.*, pp. 86–96.
14. Barker, *op. cit.*, p. 36.
15. Azeau, *op. cit.*, p. 235.
16. Robertson, *op. cit.*, p. 132.
17. Anthony Eden: *Full Circle: The Memoirs of Anthony Eden.* Houghton Mifflin, Boston, 1960, p. 509.
18. *Ibid.*, p. 573.
19. Robertson, *op. cit.*, pp. 155–163. Azeau, *op. cit.*, pp. 240–250.
20. Eden, *op. cit.*, p. 584.
21. Murphy, *op. cit.*, p. 390.
22. Eisenhower, *op. cit.*, p. 77.
23. *Ibid.*, p. 82.
24. *Ibid.*, p. 84.
25. Robertson, *op. cit.*, p. 172.
26. Eisenhower, *op. cit.*, p. 83.
27. Murphy, *op. cit.*, p. 392.

A good account of military operations is to be found in Edgar O'Ballance: *The Sinai Campaign of 1956*, Praeger, New York, 1959. For historical background, official documents, and an account of the Twenty-Two-Power London Conference, August 16–23, 1956, see Department of State: *The Suez Canal Problem*, Documentary Publication 6392, released October, 1956, U.S. Government Printing Office, Washington, D.C. For the British point of view an excellent work is D. C. Watt: *Britain and the Suez Canal*, Royal Institute of International Affairs, London, 1956. For the Egyptian point of view a sound work is Erskine B. Childer's *The Road to Suez: A Study of Western-Arab Relations*, McGibbon and Kee, London, 1962. For an impartial American point of view, consult John C. Campbell: *Defense of the Middle East: Problems of American Policy*, Council on Foreign Relations, New York, 1960. In addition to the Kimche brothers' *Both Sides of the Hill*, the most recent and authoritative Israeli account is Maj. Gen. Moshe Dayan: *The Diary of the Sinai Campaign*, New York, Harper and Row, 1966. This book was published after the present text was written.

Chapter VII
The American Landing in Lebanon, 1958

[1] This chapter is told without footnotes because "The Ambassador" is the present author. For those who are interested in further details perhaps the best eye-witness account is set forth in the first three chapters of the book *Diplomat* by Charles W. Thayer (Harper and Brothers, New York, 1959), entitled "Embassy in Crisis."

Other accounts have appeared in periodical literature. These are résuméd by reference in an excellent monograph published in 1966 by the Historical Branch, G–3 Division, Headquarters, U.S. Marine Corps, Washington, D.C., entitled *Marines in Lebanon, 1958.* Two local Marine commanders have published articles. One is entitled "Operation Blue Rat" by Brigadier General Sydney S. Wade, published in the *Marine Corps Gazette,* July 1959, pages 10–23. Another is by the lieutenant colonel who was the local commander of the first landing team, Lieutenant Colonel Harry A. Hadd, who published an article "Orders Firm But Flexible" in the *U.S. Naval Institute Proceedings,* October 1962, pages 81–89. The same issue of the *Proceedings* contained the present author's account entitled "The American Landing in Lebanon" (pages 65–79).

Both President Eisenhower in the second volume of his memoirs *Waging Peace,* and Under Secretary of State Robert Murphy in his memoirs *Diplomat Among Warriors,* have extensively commented on the Lebanon episode.

A less well-known book is by Fahim I. Qubain: *Crisis in Lebanon* (The Middle East Institute in Washington, D.C., 1961). This book provides a fairly detailed account of the Lebanese episode with extensive background material and appendices giving the U.N. debates, official statements and samples of U.A.R. and radio press attacks on Lebanon.

Chapter VIII
The Chinese Attack on the Himalayan Frontier of India, 1962

1. Dr. Satyanarayan Sinha: *China Strikes*. Blandford Press, London, 1964, p. 57.
2. *United Nations Treaty Series*. Vol. 299, 1958. No. 4307, Preamble.
   See also C. N. Satyapalan, "The Sino-Indian Border Conflict." *Orbis*, Vol. VIII, Summer 1964, No. 2, p. 376.
3. Alastair Lamb: *The China-India Border:* The Origins of the Disputed Boundaries. Oxford University Press, London, 1964, p. 14.
4. Government of India, Ministry of Information and Broadcasting: *The Chinese Threat*. New Delhi, January 1963, Map 15. Lamb, *op. cit.*, pp. 142–147.
5. Government of India, Ministry of External Affairs: *White Paper* — Notes, Memoranda and Letters Exchanged and Agreements Signed Between the Governments of India and China, 1954–1965, Vols. I–X, New Delhi. Cited hereafter as *White Paper*.
6. Government of India, Ministry of External Affairs: *Report of the Indian Officials on the Boundary Question, New Delhi, 1961*.
7. *The Hindu*, August 8, 1959, cited by Satyapalan, *op. cit.*, p. 381.
8. Satyapalan, *op. cit.*, p. 386.
   See also S. M. Burke: Sino Pakistani Relations." *Orbis*, Vol. VIII, Summer 1964, No. 2.
   Government of Pakistan, Department of Films and Publications: *Pakistan-China Boundary Agreement*. Karachi, August 1963.
9. *White Paper*, VI, pp. 96–97, 99–105, 188–222.
10. *New Statesman*, London, March 9, 1962, p. 332.
    See also Satyapalan, *op. cit.*, p. 385.
11. *White Paper*, VI, pp. 1–2.
12. *Ibid.*, pp. 3–4.
13. *Ibid.*, VII, p. 43.

14. *Ibid.*, pp. 100–102.
15. Cited in *Peking Review*, Oct. 19, 1962, pp. 6–7.
16. *White Paper*, VIII, pp. 74–78.
    Sinha, *op. cit.*, pp. 77–84.
    David T. Evans and Ray Y. Gildea, Jr.: *India and China: The Protracted Crisis.* Mississippi State College for Women, Columbus, Miss., 1963, p. 6.
17. I. O. Pub. *External Files*, 1910, Vol. 13, cited in Lamb, *op. cit.*, pp. 137–138.
18. *Ibid.*, p. 6.
    Sinha, *op. cit.*, p. 85.
19. *White Paper*, VIII, p. 19.
20. *Ibid.*, p. 49.
21. *Ibid.*, IX, pp. 184–185.
22. *Ibid.*, pp. 185–187.
23. *Ibid.*, p. 11. Chinese Note of Oct. 9, 1963.
24. Lamb, *op. cit.*, pp. 100–104, 174. Text of British Note given in Appendix II.
    Sir R. Reed: *History of the Frontier Areas Bordering on Assam from 1883–1941.* Shillong, 1942, p. 291. Cited in Lamb, *op. cit.*, p. 161.
25. Owen Lattimore: *Studies in Frontier History, Collected Papers, 1928–1958.* London, Oxford University Press, 1962, pp. 216–217.

Chapter IX
"Wars of National Liberation":
The French Colonial War in Viet Nam, 1946–1950

1. Cooper, Killigrew and La Charite: *Case Studies in Insurgency and Revolutionary Warfare: Vietnam 1941–1954.* Special Operations Research Office, The American University, Washington, D.C., 1964, p. 38. Hereafter cited as *Vietnam 1941–1954.*
2. *Ibid.*, p. 19.
3. *Ibid.*, p. 18.
4. *Ibid.*, p. 41.

5. Jules Roy: *The Battle of Dienbienphu*. Harper and Row, New York, 1965, p. 316.
6. Wilfred Burchett: *North of the 17th Parallel*. Published by the author, Hanoi, 1955. Cf. also Fall, *Le Viet-Minh*, pp. 22–33.
7. Bernard Fall: *Le Viet-Minh. La République Démocratique du Viet-Nam, 1945–1960*. Librairie Armand Colin, Paris, 1960, p. 25.
8. Général d'Armée Paul Ely: *Memoires: L'Indo-Chine dans la Tourmante*. Plon Paris, 1964, p. 102.
9. Fall, *op. cit.*, pp. 27–28.
10. *Ibid.*, pp. 29–30.
11. *Ibid.*, pp. 30–31.
12. *Ibid.*, p. 31.
13. *Ibid.*, p. 34.
   Vietnam 1941–1954, p. 106.
14. *Vietnam 1941–1954*, p. 78.
15. Fall, *op. cit.*, p. 34.
16. *Ibid.*, p. 34. See also, Robert Shaplen: *The Lost Revolution*. Harper and Row, New York, 1965, p. 30.
17. Vo Nguyen Giap: *People's War, People's Army*. Foreign Languages Publishing House, Hanoi, 1961, pp. 78–79.
18. *Vietnam 1941–1954*, p. 110.
19. *Ibid.*, p. 112.
   Fall, *op. cit.*, p. 113.
20. Philippe Devillers: *Histoire du Viet-Nam, de 1940 à 1952*, cited Fall, *op. cit.*, p. 114.
21. Alexander Werth: *France: 1940–1955*. Holt, Rinehart and Winston, New York, 1956, pp. 333–334.
22. *Vietnam 1941–1954*, p. 49.
23. Jean Santeny: *Histoire d'une Paix Manquée*. Ed. Amiot-Dumont, Paris, 1953, p. 209.
24. Bernard B. Fall: *Street Without Joy*. 4th ed., The Stackpole Co., Harrisburg, Pa., 1964, p. 27.
25. Giap, *op. cit.*, pp. 100–108.
   Vietnam 1941–1954, pp. 97–99.
26. Quoted by George A. Carver, Jr., in "The Faceless Viet Cong." *Foreign Affairs*, Vol. 44, No. 3, April 1966, p. 347.

Chapter X
"Wars of National Liberation":
The Franco-Communist War in Viet Nam, 1950–1954

1. Philippe Devillers: Histoire du Viet-Nam de 1940 à 1952. Edition du Seuil, Paris, 1952, p. 259.
2. Carver, op. cit., p. 354.
3. Dwight D. Eisenhower: The White House Years: Mandate for Change 1953–1957. Doubleday, Garden City, N.Y., 1963, pp. 170; 338.
4. Ibid., pp. 337–338.
5. Ely, op. cit., p. 33.
6. Vietnam 1941–1954, pp. 49–50.
7. Time, Vol. LV, No. 22, May 29, 1950.
8. McClintock: "U.S. Policy for Post-Armistice Vietnam." State Department, 1954.
9. Eisenhower, op. cit., p. 167.
10. Ely, op. cit., p. 25.
11. Roy, op. cit., pp. 36–37.
12. Ibid., p. 58.
13. Ibid., p. 61.
14. Ibid., p. 154.
15. Ibid., pp. 174–175.
16. Ibid., p. 188.
17. Ibid., p. 236.
18. Ely, op. cit., p. 64.
19. Ibid., p. 65.
20. Eisenhower, op. cit., p. 345.
21. Ely, op. cit., p. 66.
22. Ibid., p. 66.
23. Ibid., p. 76.
24. Ibid., pp. 84–85.
25. Roy, op. cit., p. 213.
26. Ely, op. cit., p. 90.
27. Eisenhower, op. cit., p. 347.
28. Anthony Eden: Full Circle: The Memoirs of Anthony Eden. Houghton Mifflin, Boston, 1960, p. 103.
29. Eisenhower, op. cit., p. 351.

30. *Ibid.*, pp. 350–355.
31. Roy, *op. cit.*, p. 195.
32. Eden, *op. cit.*, p. 139.
33. Department of State *Bulletin*, August 2, 1954, pp. 162–163.
34. Ely, *op. cit.*, p. 32.
35. *Ibid.*, p. 73.
36. McClintock, *op. cit.*
37. *Ibid.*
38. *Vietnam 1941–1954*, p. 119.
39. Roy, *op. cit.*, p. 12.
40. McClintock: "The River War in Indo China." *U.S. Naval Institute Proceedings*, Vol. 80, No. 12, December 1954, pp. 1303–1311.

Chapter XII
The Lessons of Limited War

1. *Time*, Sept. 24, 1965, p. 30.
2. *Ibid.*, p. 31.
3. Mao Tse-tung: *Selected Works*, Vol. II, "On the Protracted War." International Publishers, New York, 1954, p. 202.
4. Statement at Hudson Institute Seminar, October 7, 1965.
5. Thucydides III, 13.
6. As formulated by Marshall Lin Piao and published in all major Chinese newspapers, September 3, 1965. *New York Times*, Sept. 4, 1965.
7. Eisenhower: *The White House Years: Waging Peace, 1956–1961*. Doubleday, Garden City, N.Y., 1963, p. 42.
8. *New York Times*, Jan. 2, 1966.
9. Richard E. Neustadt, cited in Senator Henry M. Jackson: *The Secretary of State and the Ambassador*. Praeger, New York, 1964, p. 94.
10. Jackson, *op. cit.*, pp. 18–19.
11. Department of State: Foreign Affairs Manual Circular No. 385, March 4, 1966.
12. Edgar Snow: "Interview with Mao." *New Republic*, Feb. 27, 1965, p. 23.

Index